CHURCHILL ROCK.

PART V.

ECONOMIC GEOLOGY.

CHAPTER I.

METALS AND THEIR ORES.

ECONOMIC geology is an account of rocks with reference to their pecuniary value, or immediate application to the wants of society. A full treatise would include a description of the methods of mining, quarrying, and metallurgy; chemical processes for the manufacture of various salts; account of the manufacture of quicklime, glass, and earthenware; the discussion of the nature and origin of metalliferous deposits; the uses of peat in agriculture, etc. Our work will be mainly the description of the localities, modes of occurrence, and quantity of materials valuable for economic purposes. Very few of the industries involved in the manufacture of mineral materials have become thoroughly established in New Hampshire, so that our contributions to the perfection of the processes employed cannot be extensive. Allusion will be made from time to time to methods of manufacture or processes of reduction, so far as seems desirable. For convenience, this part will be divided into three chapters,—first, that relating to the occurrence and extraction of the metals; second, facts about the supplies of mineral materials used for building and the manufacture of useful articles; third, an account of deposits serviceable to the interests of agriculture. A part of this topic has been already discussed in the chapter upon Agricultural Geology in Volume I.

The following metals occur in considerable abundance in the state (insomuch that the question will be raised with each, whether its ores can be mined advantageously): Gold, silver, copper, iron, lead, zinc, tin, bismuth, manganese, arsenic, and molybdenum.

Gold.

Dr. Jackson discovered minute quantities of gold in the magnetic pyrites of Canaan and Enfield. He made very extensive examinations of several lots of the ore, and thoroughly satisfied himself that the metal existed in too small amount to be of any practical value.

I have had specimens sent me from a great many towns in the state, believed to contain gold, and find most of them of no value. Those who are inexperienced mistake yellow pyrites and mica for gold. In other cases, as quartz is known to carry this metal in auriferous countries, people are convinced that, if a vein of this substance is found in their neighborhood, it must be rich in gold. In Volume II we have described enormous beds or veins of this rock, some of them traceable for a hundred miles. These have been opened at several places, but have nowhere been found profitable, if, indeed, the presence of gold in small amount is not a delusion. The wishes of the proprietors, coupled with duplicity on the part of prospectors or speculators, may often lead to false reports of the presence of gold. I have seen nothing to convince me that gold exists in the following large beds or veins: The Hooksett and Manchester ranges of quartz, seen between Royalton, Mass., and Denmark, Me.; the beds in the Rockingham mica schist in Londonderry, Raymond, Northwood; the smaller patches in Concord, Holderness, Sandwich, Warner; those on the west side of the state, in Richmond, Keene, Surry, Acworth, Alstead, Croydon, Newport, Grafton, etc. Add to these the beds of quartz found in the Bethlehem, Huronian, and Coös groups.

I have notes of operations upon some of these beds. In Sandwich, some openings were made in 1877, in the "White ledge," one mile north-west of Sandwich centre, with the high-sounding name of "Diamond Ledge Gold Mine." No pure gold is visible. The operators claim an average yield of $49 to the ton.

In Ossipee, a quartz band from four to eight rods wide occurs on the south side of Pocket hill, near the house of Obed Sanders. The quartz is unusually crystalline and open, traversed by numerous veins of the same material, and also by granite. No metals or ores are seen in it.

The "silver mine" in the same town, on the land of Jonathan D. Sias, presents similar lithological features and dimensions. The metalliferous part is on the south-east wall of the quartz, separated by a width of eight inches of fuller's-earth from a trap dyke. A shaft has been sunk 36 feet. The adjoining rock is granitic gneiss. The ore is scantily disseminated through a width of four to seven feet, sometimes pinching out entirely. It consists of galena, magnetite with blue stains, copper and iron pyrites, and zinc blende. This opening was made in 1876.

In the north part of Wakefield, on the land of Ira Hammond and S. B. Ames, is a similar band of white quartz with scanty veins of galena, blende, iron and copper pyrites. Mined in 1876, and two shafts sunk to the depth of 10 and 17 feet.

In the north-west part of Strafford there is another opening in one of these beds, much talked of by the prospectors. I have seen the beds, but not the openings. The quartz is of remarkable extent and purity. I should not expect any of these "mines" to prove profitable.

The following is the report of Mr. Huntington upon the prospect of finding gold in Pittsburg, made in 1871. There is reason to believe that explorations for gold in this town may be successful:

Alluvial Gold of Indian Stream.

In that part of Quebec Province that lies between the St. Lawrence, Maine, New Hampshire, and Vermont, the existence of gold in the alluvium has been known for many years. It is estimated that the area over which it extends comprises more than ten thousand square miles. The gravel containing gold rests generally upon metamorphic schists, some of which are associated with diorites and serpentines. Mr. A. Michel compares the gold deposits of Lower Canada with those of Siberia. In the Ural and Altai mountains the auriferous gravels are almost always found reposing on schistose rocks, very rarely granitic or sienitic, as along the Pacific in North and South America. He further says, that the gold in Quebec Province, "whether in large or small grains, is generally so smooth, so much rounded and worn by friction, that it appears to come from some distance." * * * "The condition of the gold shows it to have been, for the greater part, at least, detached, rounded, and ground by erosive action of currents of water."

In the town of Ditton, which borders on New Hampshire, and is immediately north of the head waters of Indian stream, alluvial gold washing, by sluicing, has been carried on for several years. The place where the most extensive operations are is on a branch of Salmon river, three and a half miles from the boundary. The stream at first runs a little south of east, but at the point where the principal excavations have been made it turns and runs northward. So that here there is a basin in which the drift has accumulated to the depth of fifteen or twenty feet. The upper portion, which consists of a very coarse gravel and has a thickness of three or four feet, was probably deposited by the stream, and it contains no gold. The portion below consists of both coarser and finer material, from clay to boulders eight or ten inches in diameter. Through this the gold is irregularly distributed, but it is most abundant near the bed rock, which here consists of an argillaceous schist, quite fissile, and containing numerous cavities filled with a yellowish powder. This mine has been worked during the summer months every year since 1866, and from ten to twenty men have been employed by the proprietor, J. H. Pope, M. P.

As gold was found immediately north of New Hampshire, and since the drift through which it was distributed came from the northward, the drift striæ where they were noticed being S. 28° E., there is every probability that gold will be found within our limits. But prospecting in a wilderness ten or fifteen miles from the habitations of men, where the places can be reached only on foot, requires a great amount of time and labor, and therefore our explorations have not been so thorough as they might have been under more favorable circumstances.

In my explorations on Indian Stream, I employed an Indian, Mr. A. A. Annance, who was formerly a student at Hanover, but who now prefers hunting moose and trapping sable to studying calculus and reading Greek. The points examined were on and near Indian Stream, about three and a half miles from the boundary. The stream here is quite rapid, and on either side the hills rise three and four hundred feet above its bed, while every few rods, either from the east or the west, it receives a tributary. The rocks here, as elsewhere on Indian Stream, consist of argillaceous schists. These are often so wrinkled and corrugated that it is difficult to determine the dip, while elsewhere, especially where the rock is of a coarser texture, the flexures and contortions are not seen. In every respect the rocks are similar to those of Ditton. Immediately on Indian Stream the gold is chiefly found in the fissures of the schist, which is here so fragile that it is easily broken up by picks. A quarter of a mile from the stream we found the characteristic drift of this section. It consists of a bluish clayey gravel, and contains boulders of schistose rocks, and it has a depth, where we excavated, of three and four feet. The gold seems to be distributed through the entire mass, though it is nowhere very abundant; yet, when the road that was several years ago projected from Connecticut lake to the boundary is constructed, this section will be well worthy of a thorough exploration, especially as the streams are rapid, and the descent of the bed-rock is sufficient to carry away the loosened sand if the hydraulic process is used. It has been estimated* that "earth which contains only the twenty-fifth part of a grain of gold, or about two mills' worth in a bushel, will pay about two dollars a day to a pipe."—J. H. H.

The Ammonoosuc Gold Field.

Under the appellation of *Ammonoosuc Gold Field* is included the territory occupied by the auriferous slates and schists along Connecticut river, supposed to belong to the Huronian and Cambrian series, lying mostly in New Hampshire, but partly in Vermont, and possibly extending beyond the sources of the Connecticut into Maine and Canada. The southern limit is near Bellows Falls. Explorations of this field have been desultory and disconnected. The earliest discovery of free gold in any part of it, so far as can be ascertained, was made by Mr. Hanshet, in Plainfield, not later than 1854. This was but a short time before Moses Durkee, of Lebanon, washed gold out of alluvium in both Hanover and Lebanon. In the report upon the geology of Vermont,† published in 1861, Springfield, Vt., is given as a gold locality. It was obtained from the gravel, and but a short time previous, according to my note-book. No other proof of the presence of gold in the Connecticut valley is cited in that report, though its existence there is "strongly suspected."‡ In 1858, while acting as assistant on the Vermont survey, I measured a section, from Lake Champlain over Camel's Hump and Mt. Washington, which crossed this auriferous field in Littleton.§ The similarity of the ledges to those in the great talcose schist and gold-bearing formations just east of the Green Mountains led us to regard them of the same age

* *Mining Statistics west of the Rocky Mountains*, 1870, p. 478.

† Page 683. ‡ Page 849. § Page 521.

and character. In my report on the geology of Maine, I have described the supposed continuation of this formation as probably auriferous; and it may be connected with the gold rocks upon the Upper Chaudiére and St. Francis rivers of Canada, described by Sir W. E. Logan, and said to have yielded masses of gold weighing 126 pennyweights.*

The first discovery of gold in Lyman was made by Prof. Henry Wurtz, of New York, in August, 1864. Prof. Wurtz visited the locality and the neighborhood in July and September, 1864, and in December, 1866. He sent several specimens of galena to Dr. John Torrey, to be assayed, requesting that they might be tested for gold as well as silver. The third sample submitted to Dr. Torrey, coming from the Orchard vein of the New Hampshire Silver Lead Company, contained silver at the rate of 56.95 ounces, and gold at the rate of 1.006 ounces to the ton of 2,000 pounds. Wurtz's reports were issued by the Silver Lead Company in 1864; and subsequently he prepared for the *American Journal of Mining* † a full account of his connection with the discovery, and suggested very appropriately that the whole auriferous district be called the Ammonoosuc Gold Field, as it is drained by the Ammonoosuc river and its tributaries. He remarks of the Lyman district, that the "history of this gold field presents, probably for the first time, the peculiarities of a first discovery in the *solid rock,* and not, as usual, by the tracing up of gulch gold to its home in the lodes." The appropriateness of the name, coming from so high an authority as Prof. Wurtz, led us to extend it over the whole area of the group in New Hampshire and Vermont, as has been often mentioned in the previous volumes of this report.

In 1865, both J. Henry Allen and Charles Knapp, independently of each other, discovered free gold on the David Atwood estate in Lisbon. This led to the organization of the Lisbon Gold Mining Company, on the 28th of February, 1866, with a nominal capital of $240,000. Previously to this organization a little work, or "prospecting," had been done, and subsequently three considerable excavations were made in the vein. The first is in a swampy piece of land on George brook. This has been sunk to the depth of 94 feet, the first 35 vertical, and the remainder at an angle of 45° or more, upon the supposed dip. It is said that a dyke

* *Geological Survey of Canada. Report of Progress from its Commencement to* 1863, p. 437.

† Sept. 12, 1868.

of trap is connected with the vein in the foot-wall as low as fifty feet. The greatest amount of free gold showed itself within twenty-five feet of the surface. The gangue of the vein is quartz, about one twentieth part being composed of magnetic iron pyrites or pyrrhotite, with a slight sprinkling of yellow copper pyrites or chalcopyrite. The assays of the rock were said to indicate at least $60 to the ton. It is probable that the pyrrhotite contains gold, as the best specimens show free gold intermingled with it. It is estimated, by good authority, that about three hundred dollars have been obtained practically by milling from this mine.

The second opening, a few rods up the hill on the south bank, was sunk 30 feet. The third, much farther south, was sunk 25 feet. All the openings indicate a vein over four feet in thickness, similar to that already described, and bounded by a hard quartzite resembling gneiss. The vein is about an eighth of a mile removed from a clay slate.

The company were not very successful in extracting the gold from this mine, and ceased to excavate in December, 1866, allowing the opening to become filled with water. They then bought one half of what is known as the Dodge mine, and since the abandonment of the first, have wrought the second diligently. Their capital stock has been reduced to $48.000.

The Dodge Mine. In June, 1866, Mr. J. H. Barrett, while laboring on the Dodge farm in Lyman, nearly two miles by road from Lisbon village, discovered a stone projecting from the wall which contained a yellow substance resembling gold. The specimen was sent down to S. K. Fisk, of Lisbon, who pronounced the yellow mineral iron pyrites; but upon cleaning the other face of the stone discovered a large sprinkling of gold, the finest specimen ever found in New Hampshire. This discovery led to a search for the vein. Three or four shallow openings were made, and an association formed to work one half the property, known as the Dodge Gold Mining Company, with a nominal capital of $75,000. The Lisbon and Dodge companies have worked this mine jointly since the early part of 1868, each transporting its share of quartz to the mills at Lisbon village. The Dodge mill commenced operations March 12, 1868, on the north side of the river. Each mill has ten stamps, and is capable of crushing and amalgamating eight tons in twenty-four hours.

The history of the operations of the Dodge and Lisbon mines has been quite varied. The Dodge company worked the mine and milled the quartz from the date just mentioned to the last part of 1869. B. F. Martin, the president, states that the sum of $24,500 was obtained while it was under his care. For the six months from December, 1869, to June, 1870, the property was leased to E. L. Hall and John McCall. Dr. Rae says they obtained $6,570 during this time. Others estimate the amount higher,—about 30 tons per week of ore, valued at $12, for 26 weeks, making over $9,000. Messrs. Fay and Wilmarth next leased the property for six months in 1870–71, and are thought to have taken out $2,000. In the spring of 1873, Dr. Julio H. Rae leased the property, and applied a process of his own to the separation of the gold from the quartz. He claims to have taken out $3,500 in July and August of that year. He found an average of $25 to the ton at first, but afterwards only $18 was obtained. Up to the time of the formation of the Electro-Gold Mining Company, the entire amount of gold milled was $36,570. Dr. Rae says it would be proper to add $5,000 for the supposed stealings, and half as much for the value of the specimens that have been carried away.

This new company wrought the mine and mill successfully for two or three years. From several letters written by the president, Dr. Rae, I cull the following:

Under date of October 17, 1873, he writes:

Enclosed please find copy from book of one week's run, made while experimenting:

Monday, one ton gross yielded	. . . .	1550	grains	of gold.
Tuesday, " " "	. . . .	1620	"	"
Wednesday, " " "	. . . .	1850	"	"
Thursday, " " "	. . . .	2240	"	"
Friday, " " "	. . . .	1790	"	"
Saturday, 600 pounds yielded	. . . .	1220	"	"
Monday, 1750 " "	. . . .	1590	"	"
Tuesday, one ton gross "	. . . .	2000	"	"

Under date of March 25, 1874, he writes,—

Our ore has averaged $19 per ton, the finest varying from 930 to 955, gold,—silver, 42 to 65. The ore has run down to about $1.25 per ton, and the richest of which I run, probably about three tons, went as high as $95. The mean average of the ore can be safely estimated at $19 per ton, if judgment is exercised in culling. The vein being very wide—18 feet—mining is cheap; but we cull our ore about fifty per cent., making the ore cost, for mining and culling, about $2 per ton. Add $1 for cartage, and $1.50 for milling, or work in mill in reducing ore to bullion, and you will find that the cost of mining and milling is $4.50 per ton of 2,240 pounds.

The director of the U. S. Mint reports the receipts of gold from New Hampshire for the year ending June 30, 1875, to be $5,200.92. For the year following, the amount was $2,731.74. A figure given in the director's report for the amount received from New Hampshire up to the last mentioned date probably denotes the total received from the Electro-Gold company: it is $10,233.68. If this sum be added to the total known to have been extracted prior to 1873, viz., $36,570, we shall have $46,803.68 as the total amount of gold mined at Lyman prior to 1876. Mr. Willard Parker, of Lisbon, who has been familiar with the whole history of the extraction of the gold in Lyman, estimated the whole amount extracted to the same date at $48,000. The close coincidence of our two independent estimates leads to the belief in their essential correctness. There has been some gold taken from the vein since 1876, so that it may be proper to say, in round numbers, that $50,000 of the gold coin in circulation in the United States has been derived from New Hampshire during the past ten years.

The tract of land occupied by the Dodge and Lisbon companies comprises about 170 acres in the east part of Lyman, and is defined upon the map opposite page 296, Volume II. The companies are engaged in litigation at the present time rather than in the development of their mines. The land has been divided into sections of 500 feet each, that at the southern end being owned by the Dodge company, and the second by the Lisbon company; the third by the Dodge, the fourth by the Lisbon, and so on. The improvements made are upon the first sections respectively.

The Dodge mine was leased for a time to J. H. Paddock & Co., from about March 1, 1874, who used the mill upon the east side of the river at Lisbon village. I have no facts about the production of gold by this firm, nor of that obtained by the Lisbon company after the Electro-Gold company ceased to operate.

The Dodge Vein. The formation carrying the auriferous veins of this type has been described in Volume II as the Cambrian clay slate. There is little mention made of the veins, save in the catalogue of the specimens obtained from the Ammonoosuc district, and their delineation upon the map on page 296. The quartz is somewhat glassy, whitish, except where it has been stained by the decomposition of pyrites, and nearly pure. Masses of slate, crystals of pyrites, ankerite, and galena are scattered through it. It is common to find spangles of free gold in the quartz, most conspicuously at the boundary between the quartz and fragments of slate in it. The ankerite is a characteristic mineral of all the auriferous veins of the Connecticut valley clay slates.

The question arose early as to the proper source of the gold. All that can be seen macroscopically is in the clear quartz. In 1869, I had the general average of the vein assayed, and also each constituent by itself, except the galena, which was of rare occurrence. The average was taken twice;—first, a picked sample from the vein; second, a portion of several hundred pounds' weight that had been pulverized in the mill for practical extraction. According to Prof. C. A. Seely, the amount of gold in both the averaged samples was essentially the same, or $18.90 to the ton. Of the constituents examined separately, taken from the same pile, the clear quartz yielded $18.11 of gold to the ton. The pyrites occurring in the quartz and in the slate both yielded traces of gold, but not enough to be measured, the latter affording the greatest amount. Neither the slate nor the ankerite afforded any trace of gold. If it were allowable to generalize from these single determinations, it were easy to say that 95 hundredths of the gold comes from the clear quartz, and the balance from the pyrites in the vein. There is not very much of this mineral present, but sufficient to attract attention, and to be saved by some of the manipulators. Seeing a pile of this pyritiferous residue in the rooms of the Electro-Gold company's mill, I begged samples for assay. Prof. Blanpied found no gold in it. The species seems to be the common bisulphuret,—not the magnetic variety, nor mispickel, which is auriferous in this neighborhood.

The gold, as obtained from this vein, is very pure. I examined twenty-four of the returns from the mint, and found the average of them to be 916.8 parts of gold to 83.2 of silver. This is purer than the average of this metal in auriferous countries; that of California is 880 in 1000;

Australia, 925.; the Chaudiére region of Canada 885 to 900; while from Nova Scotia the gold is very nearly pure.

The method of extraction first employed is the ordinary stamp process, ten small stamps rather lighter than usual, with copper and blanket amalgamation. It is thought by those much experienced in quartz milling to have been carried on in a crude manner, yet the amount saved has been a fair percentage of the assay yield. There were two of these mills, one on each side of the river at Lisbon village.

With the advent of the Electro-Gold company the Thunder-bolt crusher replaced the stamps. The rock was heated, or partially roasted. It was then crushed dry, and the powder placed in cylinders with water and quicksilver, thirty pounds to a ton of ore. This cylinder revolves four hours, and the sands flow into a dolly tub, afterwards passing over blankets. The sulphurets are caught mostly in the tub, and saved for further treatment. The blankets catch the fine gold, and are changed every four hours. This mill could treat five tons of rock in ten hours. It was the most successful of the various methods tried in New Hampshire. It has since been used more extensively in Virginia. Being of little use for the extraction of gold from sulphurets, Dr. Rae has added a desulphurizing furnace to his works, enabling him to treat ores otherwise intractable. We present herewith the original specifications of the patent describing this process.

123,932. United States Patent Office. Julio H. Rae, of Syracuse, New York. Improvement in Voltaic Amalgamators for Gold and Silver.

Specification forming part of Letters Patent No. 123,932, dated February 20, 1872.

To all whom it may concern:

Be it known that I, Julio H. Rae, of the city of Syracuse, in the county of Onondaga and state of New York, have invented a new and useful improvement in voltaic amalgamators for ore; and I do hereby declare the following to be a full, clear, and exact description thereof, which will enable those skilled in the art to make and use the same, reference being had to the accompanying drawing forming part of this specification, in which drawing,—

Fig. 1 represents a longitudinal vertical section of my invention. Fig. 2 is a plan or top view of the same. Fig. 3 is a detached longitudinal central section of the voltaic cylinder, which forms one of the principal parts of my amalgamator, in a larger scale than the previous figure, the line *x x*, Fig. 4, indicating the plane of section. Fig. 4 is a transverse section of the same in the plane *y y*, Fig. 3. Fig. 5 is a detached section of the washer in a larger scale than the first two figures. Fig. 6 is a plan or top view of the same.

Similar letters indicate corresponding parts.

This invention consists in the arrangement of a voltaic pile in the interior of an amalgamating-cylinder in such a manner that, when said cylinder is charged with the pulverized ore, quicksilver, and proper chemicals, and then revolved, the galvanic current excited in the pile materially promotes the amalgamating process. Also, in the arrangement of a rod extending centrally through the amalgamating-cylinder, and forming the support of the voltaic pile, the copper elements of which connect with one head, and the zinc elements of which connect with the opposite head of said cylinder, in such a manner that the elements are securely retained and not liable to get out of position by the revolution of the cylinder; and at the same time the voltaic pile offers the least possible obstruction to the revolving motion of the cylinder. Further, in the arrangement of one or more voltaic cylinders in a receiving-tank which connects with an agitating-tub in such a manner that the pulp discharged from said voltaic cylinder or cylinders can be washed, and the floating particles of quicksilver contained therein can be saved. Also, in combining the voltaic cylinders, the receiving-tank, and the agitating-tub with one or more washers, composed of conical copper-lined vessels, each of which contains a hollow inverted truncated cone suspended from a water-supply pipe, and provided with a large number of small holes in the bottom and lower part of its outer shell, in such a manner that, by the up current of the jets of water discharging from said holes, the particles of mercury still mixed with the tailings received in the washer are recovered, while the tailings flow off through a copper-lined gutter, the copper lining of which retains the last traces of mercury which may be still mixed with the tailings.

3 Sheets--Sheet 1.

J. H. RAE.

Improvement in Voltaic Amalgamators for Gold and Silver

No. 123,932. Patented Feb. 20, 1872.

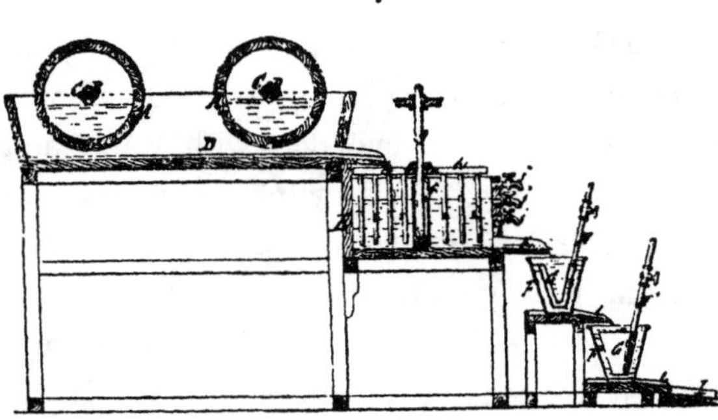

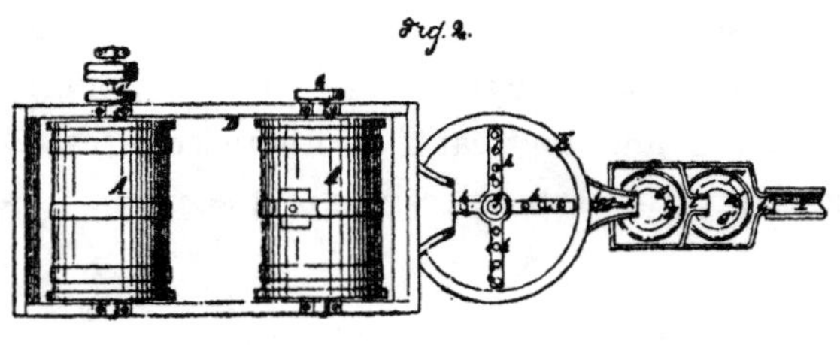

Witnesses. Inventor.

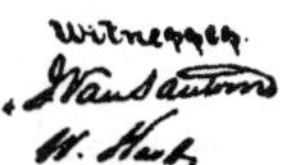

In the drawing, the letters A A designate cylinders, each of which is constructed as shown in Figs. 3 and 4 of the drawing. Through the centre of each of these cylinders extends a rod, B, the ends of which have their bearings in sockets formed on the interior of the heads of the cylinder, and on this rod are secured the elements of a voltaic pile, C. All the copper elements of this pile are connected by a wire, *a*, which is in contact with one of the heads of the cylinder, while the zinc elements are connected by a wire, *d*, which is in contact with the opposite head of said cylinder. By this arrangement I obtain a voltaic pile of great power in a comparatively small space; but it must be remarked that one or more voltaic piles might be arranged in the interior of the cylinder in any desired position, and I do not wish to be confined to the precise arrangement of the voltaic pile which I have shown. Each of the cylinders A is provided in one side with a man-hole, through which the cylinder can be charged and discharged, and which can be firmly closed by a man-hole plate *c*. Through the side of the cylinder opposite the man-hole extends a pipe, *d*, which can be opened and closed by a stop-cock, *e*, and which serves to draw off the quicksilver at the proper time, as will be hereafter more fully explained. From the outer surfaces of the heads of the cylinders project gudgeons, *e'*, which have their bearings in the edges of a tank, D, which is intended to receive the pulp and conduct it to the agitating-tub E. From the bottom of this tub rises a tube, *f*, to a level with the top edge, and this tube forms the bearing for a vertical shaft, *g*, from which extend radiating arms *h*, carrying the agitators *i*, which extend down near to the bottom of the tub E, as shown in Fig. 1. In the side of this tub are three pipes, *j*, one above the other, and each provided with a stop-cock; and from the bottom of the tub, just beneath the pipes *j*, extends the discharge-pipe *k*, which leads to the first washer F. An enlarged

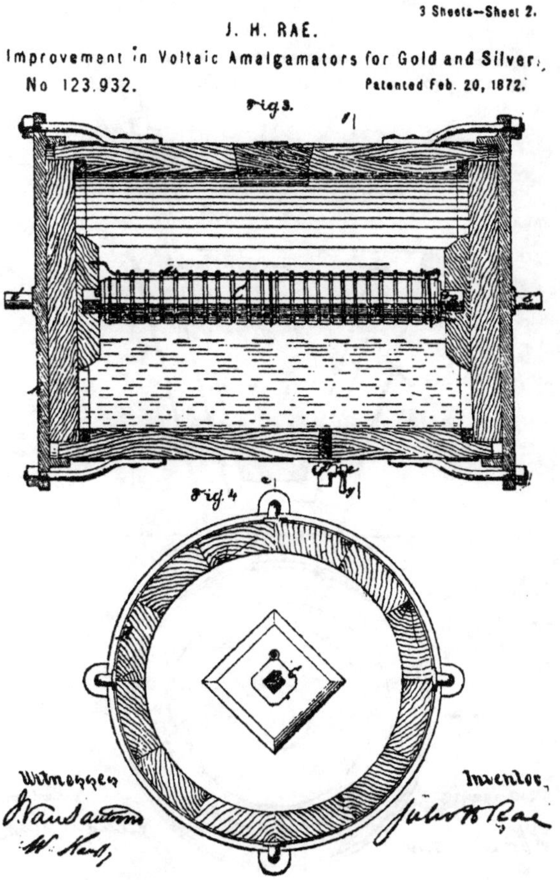

3 Sheets—Sheet 2.
J. H. RAE.
Improvement in Voltaic Amalgamators for Gold and Silver.
No 123.932. Patented Feb. 20, 1872.
Fig. 3.
Fig. 4
Witnesses
Inventor.

view of this washer is shown in Figs. 5 and 6 of the drawing. It consists of a conical tub, lined with copper, and in this tub is contained a double-walled inverted truncated cone, G, which is suspended from a water-supply pipe, H, and which is perforated with a number of small holes in its outer bottom and in the lower portion of its external jacket, so that the water admitted through the pipe H discharges from the cone G in a large number of fine jets, producing an upward current. The washer F is placed on a table, with a spout, *l*, extending over a second washer, F′, which is constructed like the first washer, and the discharge-spout *l′* of which extends over a gutter, I, lined with copper.

3 Sheets--Sheet 3.

J. H. RAE.

Improvement in Voltaic Amalgamators for Gold and Silver.

No. 123,932. Patented Feb. 20, 1872.

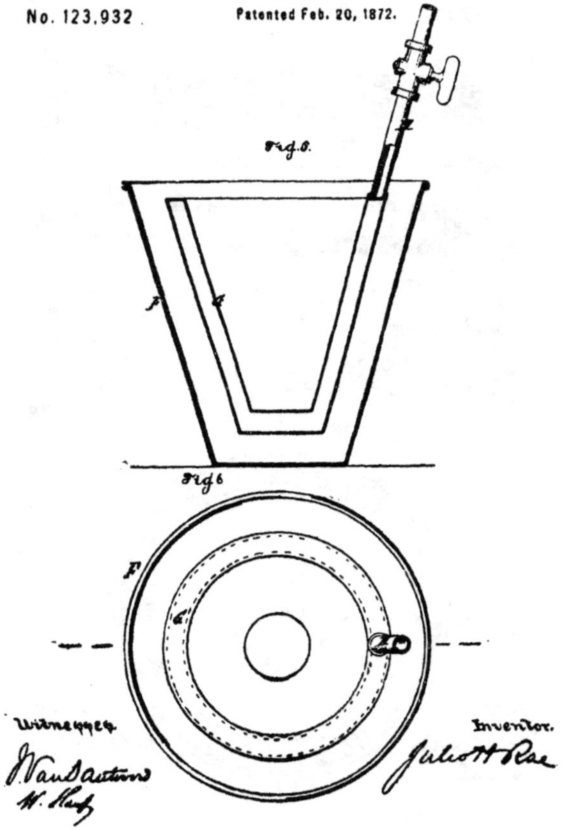

In using my invention I first reduce the ore to a fine powder, and then I introduce the same, together with a suitable quantity of water, quicksilver, and suitable exciting chemicals, into the cylinder or cylinders A. The chemicals which I use are common salt, or such acids which, when brought in contact with the voltaic pile, will excite a galvanic current. In regard to the quantity of quicksilver and the character and quantity of the exciting agent used, reference must always be had to the nature of the ore and to the electric affinities of the metals contained in the ore about to be washed. After revolving the cylinder or cylinders from three to four hours, the quicksilver is drawn off through the pipe or pipes *d*. Then each cylinder is again revolved for a few minutes for the purpose of fluidizing the pulp, when the man-hole plate is taken out, and the whole contents of the cylinder discharged into the receiving-tank D, whence the pulp gradually discharges into the agitating-tub E. In this tub the pulp is agitated, the amalgam being precipitated, while the tailings are drawn off through either of the pipes *j*, according to their specific gravity. The amalgam which collects on the bottom of the tub is removed from time to time, while the tailings pass into the first washer, F, where small particles of mercury, still mixed with the tailings, are precipitated or retained by the copper surface of the washer, while the light tailings are carried up by the up current of water produced by the jets of the cone G, and discharged over the edge of the washer F upon the table *l*, whence they run down into the second washer F′, to be treated in the same manner as above. From this second washer the tailings pass into the gutter I, the copper lining of which retains the last traces of mercury which may be still mixed with the tailings.

What I claim as new, and desire to claim by letters patent, is,—

1. The arrangement of one or more voltaic piles in the interior of an amalgamating cylinder, substantially as described.

2. The rod B, extending through the centre of an amalgamating cylinder, and supporting the elements of a voltaic pile, in combination with wires *a b*, one forming a connection between the copper, and the other between the zinc elements of the pile, substantially as set forth.

3. The arrangement of one or more voltaic cylinders in a receiving-tank communicating with an agitating-tub, substantially in the manner shown and described.

4. The combination, with one or more voltaic cylinders, a receiving-tank, and an agitating-tub of one or more washers, F F′, substantially as set forth.

5. The double-walled hollow inverted cone G, communicating with a water-supply pipe, and provided with jets in its bottom and outer jacket, in combination with a washer, F, constructed substantially as described.

JULIO H. RAE.

Witnesses:

W. HAUFF,

J. VAN SANTVOORD.

A gentleman familiar with milling has written the following sketch of the practical working of Rae's process in Virginia:

The first important difference between this and the common milling process is, that no water is introduced into the mortars, and the rock to be crushed must be perfectly dry. In all mills the degree of fineness to which the rock is powdered is regulated by a screen, through which alone the pulverized ore finds egress from the mortars.

In Rae's method, very fine screens are used, so that the rock is reduced to a very minute powder before it escapes from the batteries. It is then carried by an elevating belt to a platform above the battery, where it is emptied into a car large enough to hold one ton of crushed rock. When this amount is received, the car is removed and another placed in its stead. The car already charged with the ton of powdered rock is rolled forward till it is above the amalgamating machinery.

This consists of a large tank so inclined that fluids will readily flow from it through a vent in the lower end. Across this tank, their axis resting on journals supported by its sides, are two cylinders, each seven feet long and four feet eight inches in diameter.

On one side of each cylinder, half way between the ends, is a large opening called a manhole; on the other side, opposite, is a large faucet. By an ingenious contrivance, the manhole can be closed with absolute tightness. Inside, upon the axis of each cylinder, is a voltaic pile. Below the vent of the tank is a circular cistern, five feet in diameter and one foot six inches high, called a dolly or agitating tub. An upright shaft, standing on the centre of the bottom of this tub, is made slowly to revolve. From a horizontal cross-piece placed on this shaft, a little above the level of the top of the tub, iron teeth one foot six inches long descend. On the side of this tub opposite the vent of the tank are four holes, one above the other, through which fluid may pass into an amalgamated copper vessel, in shape an inverted hollow truncated cone. In the centre of this copper vessel, called a washer, is a hollow sphere pierced with small holes. In this sphere terminates a water-pipe connected with a reservoir above, and provided with a stopcock to regulate the flow and pressure of the water. Below this washer is another, smaller, but in every respect similar in shape and arrangement. Such is the amalgamating machinery. The amalgamation is effected as follows: From the car above the machinery the pulverized ore is, by a shute, emptied into one of the cylinders through the manhole. Water is then introduced till the cylinder is two thirds full. Any necessary chemicals, and from fifty to one hundred pounds of quicksilver, according to the richness of the ore, are added at the same time. The manhole is then closed so tight that nothing can escape; and the cylinder is revolved from three to four hours. Then the faucet is opened, and ninety to ninety-five per cent. of the quicksilver runs out into a vessel ready to receive it. Another vessel is substituted for this, and receives a large portion of the amalgam. The remaining contents of the cylinder are then allowed to flow out into the tank, and are washed down into the dolly-tub, where they are constantly agitated by the teeth on the cross-piece before mentioned. From this tub they pass into the washers, in which the jets of water from the holes in the hollow sphere keep the mass constantly in movement, so that any amalgam quicksilver or gold which shall have escaped from the cylinder and the dolly-tub sinks to the bottom of the first, or, at any rate, of the second washer.

The Dodge shaft was sunk 17 feet in 1867; and the rock taken from it yielded $6.25 per ton in the mill. After that, the whole vein on both sides was excavated for a length of several rods to the same depth, the rock yielding only $3 or $4 per ton. After the return to sinking the original shaft, $10 per ton was obtained immediately; and the yield for about two years subsequently was nearly the same, averaging $14, and in one instance reaching $19. The shaft had been excavated to a depth of about 70 feet in 1869; and there are drifts at about 60 feet depth in both directions, particularly to the east. The vein is 16 feet wide here. The rock from this depth seems to have been most productive. It is probable that not less than one fourth or one fifth of the total amount of gold present in the vein has been lost in the milling process, so that the actual results obtained do not fairly represent the true value of the rock.

Since 1869 three shafts have been sunk upon this vein, two of them to the depth of 100 feet, the third about half as much. The quality of the rock at various parts of the shafts and cuttings is not uniform. Some who have engaged in milling the quartz became discouraged on account of the small yield. By protracting on a scale, when the facts were fresh in my mind, the rich and poor portions of the quartz, I discovered a uniform method of arrangement. The richer portions occupy a definite part of the vein called a "shoot" or "chimney" by miners. The vein-sheet dips north-west, but the chimney dips to the north-east. It cannot be distinguished in the rock except by those handling it every day. In other kinds of metaliferous veins this phenomenon is very distinct, showing itself in a swelling of the mass, forming a *bonanza*. The thickness of the quartz vein is constant, and where it increases in richness the bulk is the same as before. The best method of discovering the rich and lean ore is by experiment.

There is a second quartz vein upon these properties, about eighty feet to the north, but it has not proved productive. Excavations made to the south-west upon the first Dodge lot have shown the presence of the original vein nearly to the edge of the property.

I learn that operations upon this vein are to be resumed immediately, or in the spring of 1878.

Other Quartz openings. A few other veins similar to the above occur in Lyman and its vicinity. One of the most noted is the Bedell mine, about a mile farther west. The mineralogical character is the same as that just described. It is two feet wide. Specimens showing much free gold are easily obtained. I panned out several pieces of gold from a shovelful of earth scraped from the top of the ledge, and saw much richer yields in the hands of others. A reliable assay of it in 1869 showed $12 to the ton of gold present. There is more galena than usual in the vein, carrying $33 of silver to the ton. A shaft has been sunk to the depth of 20 feet.

Near the Haviland copper mine is the Hartford or Moulton mine. A shaft has been sunk about 100 feet. At the depth of 23 feet the quartz vein, not of much width, is said to have assayed $30 in gold and $10 in silver to the ton. I have seen specimens of free gold from this mine.

Other openings are upon the clay slate area close to the conglomerate near stakes V 14 and 15 (Vol. II, p. 296), or the Bartlett mine; the west part of Jason Titus's farm in Lyman; upon B. Dow's land, near stakes B 19 and 20; and in Bath, near the east border of the slate area. Here Smith brook falls over a ledge, at whose base is a tunnel, about twenty feet long, made many years since. I found a few specks of free gold in the quartz in small veins just below the tunnel. Other quartz veins have been recognized while collecting specimens in the field, none of which are known to be auriferous by actual test.

Gold in the Conglomerate. Attention was very early called to the presence of gold in the interesting band described with minuteness in Volume II as the auriferous conglomerate. It is regarded as older than the veins in the clay slate, and for that reason perhaps is not so rich. No extensive excavations have been made in this rock, but it is very commonly slightly auriferous. Almost every section of it will furnish auriferous samples. Authentic assays have been made from several localities, such as the following:

A sample from the field north of the Cook and Brown mine (Hiram Knapp's land), afforded to Prof. Seely gold at the rate of 90 cts. to the ton. Another determination from a neighboring locality showed 75 cts. to the ton. A well known auriferous ledge of this sort is at the house of Jacob Williams. A ledge of quartzose conglomerate crops out by the roadside, perhaps forty feet high and equally thick. This ledge, two hundred and eighty-two feet in length, is one outcrop of a very interesting division of the gold rocks, whose windings and faultings have been carefully studied by us and represented upon both our maps. It is an ancient gravel, now consolidated, but it is not known whether the gold was deposited in the original placer, or introduced in small veins at the subsequent period of elevation. The company's statement represents that assays of from six to eight hundred pounds of rock have given them from five to seven dollars* of gold to the ton, and on account of the facility with which thousands of tons can be obtained from the mass, think that an average yield at these rates would be remunerative. The

* In one case, $9.99 in currency. The latest experiment shows $3 per ton.

whole width is traversed by segregated veins in which pyrites and ankerite are abundant, while specks of galena and copper have been seen.

An opening once greatly talked of is situated on the Steery farm east of Williams's. It has been known as the "Dow ledge" at the Pittsburg mine. It is a cliff of the same conglomerate, 50 or 60 feet high, and has been opened slightly.

On the most eastern band of this rock is the "Gordon mine." There are conspicuous masses of pryites, probably magnetic, in this opening upon the top of the hill. Only a few blasts have been put in here. The conglomerate has assayed from $3 to $10 to the ton. On the west side of the crest of this hill a larger excavation has been made in a better appearing part of the rock.

What I conceive to be the same conglomerate has recently been discovered in the edge of Landaff, about a mile and a half east of Lisbon village, and known latterly as the Allen mine. The ledges of it are exposed upon the "poor-" or town-farm for more than half a mile in length, with the usual north-east strike of the country, dipping 50° or 60° north-westerly. Upon this farm are several alternations of rock,—five or six of quartz, four of slate, two of conglomerate, and a siliceous limestone, possibly encrinital. The county rock is regarded as the lower part of our Huronian, though resembling the Lyman group. The most valuable vein here is from two to four feet wide, carrying much of a dark pyrites, staining the hands. Much free gold has been found in it. I have visited it twice, and obtained gold readily by washing the crushed selected fragments. I saw three small excavations. More recent cuttings have been made; and the parties interested claim that the quartz averages about $30, while the selected specimens of pyrites have yielded at a rate of $700 to the ton. They have uncovered the vein for a distance of 100 feet, and excavated occasionally to the depth of 8 feet. The gold occurs mostly in small grains in the decomposed rock, in company with a little galena.

The same conglomerate I have discovered north of the Atwood mine, and it is undoubtedly continuous to the similar outcrop on Salmon Hole brook (Vol. II, p. 324). It runs towards the coarser conglomerate of North Lisbon. It is claimed to extend in the other direction—the south-west—towards North Haverhill.

The Grafton Company.

One of the curiosities of mining in New Hampshire has been illustrated by the history of the Grafton Gold Mining Company, organized near the beginning of the year 1869. The property is near the west corner of Lyman. It was first known as the Davis & Thayer, and afterwards as the Wiggin & Davis property. I visited it September 14, 1868, and May 10, 1869. It lies in the Huronian rocks east of Gardner's mountain, the material being dolomitic and somewhat slaty. At the surface three veins, each about a foot in width, showed themselves, with narrow slaty partings, which became smaller at 25 feet, and are said to have entirely disappeared at the depth of 76 feet,—the bottom of the shaft,—and to be 8 feet wide. The veins incline south-easterly 55° at the surface, and 10° less at the depth of 25 feet, the lowest point at which I have seen it. The vein is of limpid quartz, with many crystals of quartz, dolomite or ankerite, iron pyrites, and galena, besides some free gold, the latter most abundant in the upper vein. An immense number of segregated quartz veins ramify through the dolomitic mass that is brought to the surface.

From several statements shown me by officers of the company, it appears that the earlier assays gave over $7 of gold to the ton of rock; and at the depth of 76 feet, out of a mass weighing 50 pounds, Dr. Torrey, of New York, obtained gold at the rate of $62.17 to the ton, and of silver, $1.33. An examination of the pyrites showed no gold present. About forty per cent. of the gangue was shown to be of quartz, and the balance chiefly dolomitic. A careful examination of a similar sample by T. C. Raymond, of Cambridgeport, Mass., gave the following result: Silica, 30.3; protoxide of iron, 6.27; lime, 20.6; magnesia, 11.17; carbonic acid, 32.11;—total, 100.44. This composition led the company to believe that the pulverized rock might be used advantageously as a fertilizer after the extraction of the gold; and some experiments were instituted to show its value.

The proprietors drove a thriving business in selling this pulverized siliceous dolomite for a fertilizer. Even those reputed agricultural writers of eminence became interested, and saw great benefits to the soil in the application of this powder. No doubt some benefit came, from the fact that finely divided materials have the power of absorbing moisture from the air; but such unscientific statements as appeared in the testimonials foreshadowed the withdrawal of the substance to serve for a fertilizer. The following extracts will illustrate:

Dear Sir: I very gladly write you a statement of the effects of the "Grafton Fertilizer" as seen in my garden. Two quarts of "Fertilizer" were placed about the roots of a grape-vine which had never borne more than a plateful. It is covered with bunches of fruit now of a very large size, which will ripen much earlier than usual. I think the chemical properties contained in this "Fertilizer" will serve to hasten the period of ripening of all fruits and vegetables. Melons, cucumbers, and squashes flourish finely under its influence. Last year the vines were riddled by the striped bug; this season, when they appeared, handfuls of the "Fertilizer" were scattered over the vines, and they rapidly "vamoosed the ranch." Not one bug remained! We gathered the first cucumbers grown in the town. Melon vines are a mass of yellow blossoms and green fruit, and they are not usually prolific so far north.

The "Fertilizer" is death to all the insect tribe. Carbonic acid is fatal to animal life, while it is highly essential to the growth of the vegetable world. The "Grafton Fertilizer" possesses 32.11 per cent. of this desirable constituent,—solidified,—which, added to the lime, protoxide of iron, and silica contained therein, must prove one of the most valuable mixtures hitherto discovered.

For peach-trees, it will undoubtedly be of eminent service. The peach borer can, by its aid, be driven from its haunts, and the pear-blight remedied.

The success of this fertilizer led E. C. Stevens, of Lisbon, to provide a similar material from Lyman, which also had a considerable sale. An analysis of it shows it to contain,—Silica, 90.60; lime, 3.27; sesquioxide of iron, 3.06; alumina, .31; magnesia, .38; carbonic acid, 1.35; water, 1.06; alkalies, a trace; gold, a trace.

Gold in the Sulphurets.

Scarcely any topic connected with mining in New Hampshire is of greater practical value than the presence of gold in the various sulphurets, particularly those utilized for the extraction of lead or copper. It may frequently be the case that the expenses of mining will be just about met by the sales of copper or lead, with little or no margin for profit. Should it appear that gold or silver may also be extracted from these ores, this fact may insure a profit where otherwise none could be obtained. In other auriferous districts, gold is often obtained in abundance from sulphurets, and requires peculiar processes for its extraction. I have many statements of proprietors and prospectors, to the effect that our sulphurets are auriferous and argentiferous. If they are assuredly correct in their estimates of value, a wide field is opened for profitable investment. Several circumstances must qualify the value of the estimates made:—First, all chemists do not agree in obtaining the comparatively large results asserted by some. We have to consider whether this is the result of greater skill, on the one hand, or, on the other, to a readiness to stimulate their business. Second, the specimens assayed are usually the best of their kind. Third, if several trials have been made, the proprietor usually mentions only the best, neglecting to state how many have proved unfavorable. We should, however, remember that the precious metals may occur in chimneys throughout the sulphuret veins as well as in the quartz, so that it is easy to explain a varying richness in them.

First of all, is the statement of Prof. Wurtz, previously quoted, that galena at the east base of Gardner's mountain contains $18.63 of gold to the ton of sulphuret. This ore is not very abundant,—not sufficiently so to be worth working, in the estimate of the present proprietor. Several of the copper properties along the Gardner Mountain range have been found to contain gold, up to $15 to the ton, by Prof. F. L. Bartlett, of Portland, Me. Such are the Stevens mine in Bath, and the Gardner Mountain mine in Littleton. I have had a similar statement as to the value of the Paddock copper ore, from C. H. Crosby.

A friend of mine interested in this question has investigated it quite thoroughly for his own satisfaction. It had been stated that the Vershire copper ore frequently carried $60 of gold to the ton. Others claimed a higher figure. He selected for the test a beautiful piece of iron and copper pyrites from Corinth, as rich as any that could be found, and apparently perfectly free from silica. It was placed in the hands of a skilful analyst, with a full statement of the question at issue. In order to ensure accuracy, the best method of analysis, at double price, was employed. The report states that the amount of gold contained in the Corinth ore is 27-100 of an ounce to the ton of 2,000 pounds. This would be, in round numbers, about $5 to the ton. The result is valuable, both disposing of the wild statements afloat as to the great richness of many of our sulphurets, and indicating that the Vermont copper ores are somewhat auriferous. I think I have been told that the Vershire copper ore has been tested by the company many times, and that it may be relied upon to furnish $7 in gold to the ton. J. W. Cleaveland, of the Copperas Hill works in Strafford, informs me that several dollars' worth of gold to the ton have been found in the refuse heaps of his establishment, and a much larger amount in the fresh specimens of copper ore.*

Capt. Edgar has stated that the zinc blende of Warren carried $60 of gold to the ton. This has not been verified in a practical way.

An interesting question, of both theoretical and practical interest in this connection, relates to the chemical condition of the gold in the sulphurets. Is it a sulphuret, or the element itself, free from all combination, as in the quartz veins? The fact of the absence of any free gold in the pyrites, and its sudden appearance after decomposition, led one modern author to revive the ancient alchemistic notion of the derivation of gold from the baser metal. It is said by chemists that the pente-sulphide of potassium has no effect upon free gold, but will dissolve the sulphuret. This reagent has been brought to bear upon auriferous sulphurets, with the results claimed; and hence it seems evident that the gold occurs in pyrites in combination with sulphur. This latter element needs to be carefully eliminated from all gold-bearing ores before the precious metal can be amalgamated.

Cook and Brown's Mine. In 1875 I found renewed activity upon the opening called the Cook and Brown mine, by parties known under the name of the New England Mining and Reduction Company. About five tons of the ore had been worked in Boston, yielding $23.59 to the ton; and they desired to test certain improved processes for extracting gold from its combination with sulphur. Before thoroughly testing the vein, the mill was erected just above Young's pond; and after its completion, owing to irregularities in the vein, not enough ore could be raised to supply the works. A very few feet below the surface, a quartz vein

* He says,—"We have found that the yellow deposit from the water flowing out of the adit contains gold in small quantities. It has been known for several years that the ore from this mine contains gold; but I was not aware that we had silver until Prof. Bartlett, of Portland, Me., made an assay of some of the old spent heaps, and found, from the top of a heap that has been undisturbed for twenty years, that it contained four dollars and fifty-five cents' worth of silver and ten dollars of gold to the ton. H. F. Carpenter, of Portsmouth, R. I., has been experimenting with the pyrites for the past year, and reports that, from seventy-five to one hundred trials, he is able to get sixty dollars of gold per ton; but the gold is an ore, and not in condition to be extracted profitably." April 11, 1878.

about ten inches wide was cut into, showing free gold, and that in respectable quantity. The vein was followed down, and, with several feet of the adjoining rock, proved to be highly auriferous. Mr. Hawes's assay of samples selected by me showed the presence of 20 ounces of silver, and 2.5 ounces of gold to the ton. Trial with a pan revealed considerable gold before the decomposition of the pyrites, and much more after calcination. From $70 to $80 to the ton seemed to be a common yield, judging by the eye. The material examined was a soft, argillitic schist, full of crystals of arsenical pyrites. Massive layers of this same mineral an inch thick had been noticed in the quartz vein.

After descending 25 or 30 feet, the vein and its accompanying auriferous bands disappeared, and has never been found again, and consequently mining operations ceased. This opening is almost on the line of fault described in Volume II, page 305. The magnitude of the throw—nearly 1,200 feet—shows that the disappearance of the vein by faulting is not singular; but the richness of the auriferous deposit would render it desirable to search for its continuation.

The presence of so much gold with arsenical pyrites, here and at the Atwood and Allen mines, has suggested to me the probability that this may indicate the natural affinities of the metal in this district. The formation in which the Cook and Brown mine is located is the Lyman group,—unlike the Dodge vein in the clay slate. Future explorers will do well to remember these facts, and not neglect the arsenical ores, as they may prove to be the best in the state.

The mill has been abandoned, after it was discovered that the supply of auriferous material from this mine could not be depended upon. A lot of fifty tons of auriferous mispickel from Ontario was afterwards milled in it, apparently successfully.

The following sketch of the Crosby process is taken from a prospectus issued by the company owning the mill.

The Crosby mill contains 1 engine of 50 horse-power; 1 donkey-engine, 10 horse-power; 1 Dodge crusher; 1 pair Cornish rolls; 3 roasting cylinders; 4 Burr mills; 4 amalgamating tubs; 4 washing tables,—besides elevator, quicksilver strainers, etc.

The ore is pulverized by passing through the Dodge crusher and through the Cornish rollers. The pulverization is however incomplete, a large part of the ore going through, as gravel cannot be thoroughly roasted, and must cause loss. A dry stamp-mill would crush the rock perfectly, or perhaps an additional pair of rollers might answer the purpose. From the rollers the ore is carried as a powder to the roasting cylinders. These cylinders are made of boiler-iron, and are placed in an almost horizontal position on friction rollers, and heated to redness from the outside. Inside the cylinders are flanges or shelves fixed to the shell, and running parallel with its axes. The ore drops in at the feed end; and as the cylinder revolves, is lifted by the flanges, dropped, and thoroughly stirred. From the declination of the cylinder, the ore slowly works its way down to the discharge end, roasted or desulphurized.

The ore is now cooled, ground to a fine powder in the burrhstone mills, washed, to free it from soluble metallic salts, and amalgamated. The amalgamation is performed in tubs provided with stirrers; and by an ingenious arrangement the quicksilver is strained, the amalgam separated, and free quicksilver continuously passed in a fine shower through the pulp in the tank.

To test the efficiency of the process, I caused 174 pounds of sulphuretted ore, assaying $56.15 in gold, to be worked, and obtained 80 per cent. of the assay. Had the ore been properly crushed previous to roasting, the returns must have been larger. The powdered ore was of all degrees of fineness, from a fine powder to a gravel the size of coffee beans. Of course the latter were not desulphurized; and that we should obtain 80 per cent. of the gold with such imperfect crushing was a matter of surprise. The cost of reduction at Gold Hill, N. C., the mill working 18 tons a day, and allowing one dollar per ton for wear and tear, is $3.27½ per ton.

GEORGE CLENDEN, JR.

The results of twelve different trials with the same apparatus are also given in the prospectus. The sum total was 96 tons; the product was $1,629.29; the average value of the sampled assay, $17.69; and the product, 80 per cent. of the assay value.

ALLUVIAL WASHINGS.

In all gold-bearing countries it is common to resort to the hydraulic process for the extraction of the precious metal. Two circumstances have stood in the way of its use in New Hampshire, where it might serve an excellent purpose: first, the land in the Ammonoosuc field is valuable for farming purposes, and the farmers do not desire to have it torn up; second, there were operations of this nature upon Salmon Hole brook in Lisbon, in 1866, whose managers "salted" the sluice-boxes, and thus falsely obtained a large yield. There is no reason why a judiciously selected locality would not furnish profitable results, particularly in Pittsburg, where the value of the land is but a trifle.

Hydraulic processes have been thoroughly perfected in California. Canals, many miles in length and passing over ravines 200 feet deep, have been constructed to convey the water, so that by a large hose-pipe it may be brought to bear upon the auriferous gravel in the right place. That gravel is commonly as hard as rock, the pebbles being too firmly set to be broken apart by hand. Detailed descriptions of the processes are unnecessary; but I will mention the cost of excavation in different parts of the country, as presented by several experts. Prof. W. P. Blake estitated, from work done in North Carolina in 1859, that earth containing only the twenty-fifth part of a grain of gold, or two mills' worth in a bushel, will pay about two dollars a day to a single pipe. In California, about 1868, the same gentleman estimated that, with certain conveniences described, 1,500 tons of earth could be removed in a day's time with the labor of two men. This result has been actually obtained there under favorable circumstances.

M. Laur, a French engineer, estimating miners' wages at twenty francs ($3.68) per day, found that the expense of manual labor necessary for working one cubic metre (38 inches) of gravel by the several methods to be the following: By the pan, about $13.80; by the rocker, about $3.68; by the long tom, about $0.92; by the sluice, about $0.31; by hydraulic washing, about $0.051. This would make the cost of a cubic yard about five cents. These estimates include the cost of the water.

The cost of hydraulic mining in our state ought not to be greater than in California. These estimates do not cover the cost of the canals and apparatus, though they do include the rents paid for the water, or the interest upon the capital. The profit arising from the employment of the hydraulic processes must depend upon the richness of the gravel and the expense of uncovering the "pay dirt." In Canada, as already stated, and in Vermont, the hydraulic methods have been employed successfully within the past dozen years.

Can Gold-Mining be made Profitable in New Hampshire?

We now possess the data needful to enable us to answer this question. After ten years' intimate acquaintance with all that has been done in the way of mining and milling gold in our state, I am satisfied that this business, if properly conducted, cannot fail to be remunerative. This is not true of any regions except the Ammonoosuc district, and the related rocks along the upper Ammonoosuc river and near the border of Canada. Several points of interest in this connection may be mentioned.

First. It is not intended, when it is said the gold business ought to be remunerative, that a multitude of people can engage in it and become wealthy in a short period. A false impression prevails as to the nature of gold deposits. In California, persons have been fortunate enough to strike "pockets" of gold in the gravel containing many thousand dollars' worth of metal. Those are the few and rare exceptions. Out of the hundreds of gold quartz mines wrought upon the Pacific side of the continent, there are no instances of similar "finds." The gold is obtained only through persevering, tiresome labor. Whatever will be obtained in our state, must come in the same way. No rich placer deposits have ever been discovered within our limits. Should any such be found, and the cost of their discovery be estimated, it will appear, as is the case with those in the West, that a fair proportion of labor has been expended for the result.

Second. We must not expect to obtain profitable results in gold mining without the expenditure of considerable capital. This is like all other business pursuits. For example: a farmer must purchase land, build houses, barns, buy horses, cows, sheep, etc., procure implements of tillage, etc., before he can produce articles of merchandise. He may expend, say, $6,000, which is his capital stock. He will not expect to realize from the sales of his produce the whole amount of his investment the first year. If he obtains produce worth one thousand dollars, he would do remarkably well. So in mining and milling gold, no one ought reasonably to expect to receive the first year a larger proportionate return upon his investment than the farmer has received from his capital,—say 16 per cent. The nominal capital of the Dodge and Lisbon companies is $123,000. During the ten years of their existence, $50,000 in gold has been obtained from them. This certainly represents more than the sum of actual payments in cash by the companies, and at the least showing would indicate a 4-per cent. annual dividend for the whole time.

The question arises, What is the proper capital required to carry on successfully a single mining and milling establishment in New Hampshire? The first item is the cost of the land, by lease or fee simple. This is a matter of special agreement between buyer and seller. I will assume that a section of the Dodge or Lisbon mine, 500 feet in length, or one of equal value elsewhere, may be obtained for $5,000. The cost of a mill-site depends upon the same considerations as that of the mine. Suppose the site and improvements, with buildings, to cost $8,000. The necessary machinery, such as that used most recently in Lisbon, can be put in by responsible parties for $2,500. Add $1,000 for opening the mine and various necessary expenses, and the amount of capital required, therefore, for the establishment throughout, would be about $16,500. The working expenses may be determined by what has been paid already. In 1875, the Lisbon company paid $1.50 per ton for mining, and $1 for the delivery of the rock at the mill. The Electro company, in 1874, paid for mining and culling $2 per ton, $1 for cartage, and $1.50 for milling. In 1869, I stated that the cost of mining and cartage was about $4 to the ton, and the expense of milling about the same, or $8 in all. This was estimated in a depreciated currency, and before the art of mining was well understood in Lyman. I suppose the first two estimates do not include the cost of superintendence.

Some of the best estimates of the cost of gold mills and of working them in California are given in R. W. Raymond's report on the *Mineral Resources west of the Rocky Mountains* for 1872. The cost of a complete mill, including engine and boiler, is usually estimated at $1,000 per stamp. In a large mill of as many as 20 stamps, this includes the concentrating and chlorination works. The same authority presents a detailed account of the entire cost of milling, including interest on the cost, repayment of cost, and management. In a 30-stamp steam-mill, with a crushing capacity of 72 tons a day, this expense is $2.04 per ton, not including the cost of concentrating the tailings and chlorinating the concentrates. The last item would not be of much account when very few sulphurets are found. It would correspond to the expense of working the sulphurets, such as was incurred in the Crosby mill in Lyman. I understand the entire cost of that mill to have been $18,000, and to be capable of working 20 tons of ore per diem. Mr. Crosby estimated the entire expense of milling to be $5 per ton, and $2 additional for mining and delivery,—making $7 in all.

Using these figures for a basis, and making allowances for apparatus and superintendence, the following may express the proper capital and working expenses for extracting the gold from the two classes of ore occurring in New Hampshire:

	Quartz mining.	Sulphurets.
Cost of mine,	$5,000	$5,000
Cost of mill,	10,500	18,000
Opening the mine,	1,000	1,000
Total capital,	$16,500	$24,000

Running expenses.	Quartz mining.	Sulphurets.
Mining and cartage, per ton,	$3.00	$3.00
Milling, per ton,	2.00	5.00
Superintendence, say—	.10	.10
	$5.10	$8.10

Should a company be formed to extract gold from the quartz or sulphurets, these figures express the capital absolutely necessary for the undertaking and the proper running expenses. Circumstances of various kinds might add to or diminish the amount of necessary capital; but there would not be much variation from the figures given for the running expenses.

It is easy, from these figures, to estimate the income which might be obtained from a single enterprise of this nature. If the ore averaged as high as $19 per ton, as stated by Dr. Rae, the profit on each ton milled should be $14.90. Eight tons were carried through the whole process daily in 1875. That should afford a daily profit of $119.20. Supposing that the daily yield be practically $15, which was the case in the earlier workings, and allowing $10 per ton for the net income, we should have $80 as the daily return to the company, or $20,000 for the year of 250 working days. These figures are indications of what the gold mining business might become in our state when properly and economically conducted. A larger capital, mills of greater capacity, and the reduction of a greater number of tons daily, by employing night labor, would add very much to the amount realized. I have not given the results obtained from working the sulphurets. Those given from essentially actual experience are to be preferred; and they will afford a method of estimating the possible merits of the gold mining and milling business.

SILVER.

Several veins of galena afford valuable percentages of silver. The only one that has been milled is from Madison. According to Prof. Seely's assay, this contains 94 ounces, 11 pennyweights, and 5 grains of silver to the ton of lead. This is the old Eaton mine described by Jackson. I understand, from the late H. J. Banks, the manager of the mine, that during his administration $55 per ton was obtained by actual sale for the silver contained in the ore. The mine itself will be described under lead.

Near the summit of the road over Gardner's mountain, in the southwest corner of Lyman, are veins of argentiferous galena, owned by J. H. Paddock, of St. Johnsbury, Vt., which have been exploited slightly, and are worthy of further attention. I examined them first in 1869. The earth and a little rock were removed, exposing a vein of clear pyrites and galena over four inches thick. This was traced for five or six rods, cutting the strata at an angle of 70°, the dip of the strata being 62° easterly, and the vein 50° S. 20° E. In 1875 I found that additional excavation had uncovered the vein down to 16 inches in width, the principal portion being galena. Returns from the assay office show from $15 to $36 of silver to the ton.

One of the first mines opened in Lyman showed both silver and gold in the galena. It is not worked for either of these metals at present. The property is a part of the Paddock company, and had originally the name of the New Hampshire Silver Lead Company, with a nominal capital of $500,000. From Prof. Wurtz's reports upon this property, made in 1864, I have condensed the following statements:

There are two groups of veins, called the West lodes and Orchard veins, the former cupreous, the latter of lead and silver. The west group consists of three "heavy quartz outcrops," one of them, 10 feet wide, containing numerous strings and bunches of galena, with copper pyrites, gossans, and honeycombed cavities, including "*vugs*," or cavities lined with crystals of quartz, rarely containing indigo copper. It was traced 300 or 400 yards in length. The schists adjacent are greatly stained and incrusted with limonite or iron ore, indicating a highly metalliferous condition for the country.

The second, or Orchard group of veins, consists of two, each about two feet wide, and apparently true fissure veins, with the compass course N. 50° E. They contain chiefly galena and zinc blende. The quartz is "comby," carrying much gossan; and the walls, which near the surface are very rotten, become hard and quartzose several feet down, and well charged with iron pyrites. Several assays of the different galenas have been made by Dr. Torrey, and the results tabulated as follows. He supposes the galena to contain only 80 per cent. of pure lead, allowing for impurities; and the ton is taken at its full value of 2,240 pounds.

	Ounces of silver.	Ounces of gold.	Value of silver in coin.	Value of gold in coin.	Total.
In 1 ton of galena from					
West lode—dark	55.877	....	$72.24	....	$180.00
" light	35.716	....	46.18	....	154.00
Mean of west lode	45.798	....	59.21	....	167.00
Orchard vein	51.027	0.9014	65.98	$18.63	192.50
Mean of the three	47.540	....	61.43	....	175.50

An adit has been driven 300 feet into the hill to drain the west lodes.

Argentiferous galena has recently been discovered by Capt. F. Bennett, superintendent of the Paddock mines, at both the 60- and 120-feet levels, and from the shaft to the end of the drift, a distance of some 60 feet. It occurs continuously along the foot-wall of the copper beds in considerable amount. The best assays show the presence of 89 ounces of silver to the ton, worth $89.73 at present prices. The value of this discovery consists in the fact that all the silver and lead found will be put to the account of profit, as the copper will meet the expenses of mining.

The Stevens copper mine in Bath has a vein of argentiferous galena upon it, separate from the copper, about 18 inches wide. It is said to carry fifty dollars' worth of silver to the ton. I do not know of any other instances of silver in the Gardner Mountain range; but its importance will lead the proprietors of the other mines to search for it. The facts stated about its occurrence are sufficient to justify further exploration; and it will not be strange if the further developments would make the silver business more prominent than the copper mining.

Farther east in Lyman, mention has already been made of galena in the gold mines. That from the Bedell mine is said to yield thirty-three dollars' worth of silver to the ton. In the Dodge, Hartford, and Titus properties it also occurs, but not extensively. It should always be saved, as it is argentiferous, if not auriferous also. Any of the lead ores in the state are likely to prove argentiferous. Such are at Warren, Shelburne, Hooksett, Rumney, and Woodstock, besides recently discovered outcrops in Madison.

In this connection, I will present a brief sketch of the famous silver mine of Newburyport, Mass., just over the New Hampshire line. It was discovered in 1874. The high prices paid for lands in the neighborhood have excited the minds of many of the inhabitants of Rockingham county; and specimens of lead, pyrites, or mispickel found in that part of the state have been carefully preserved, and the ledges exploited. I have examined several openings in that county, as in Newmarket, Exeter, Epping, Fremont, and Raymond, but have not seen anything of value. The veins are of quartz, with a little pyritous ore, imbedded in one of the schistose formations. The Newburyport mine is in sienite; and therefore one would look for corresponding veins in the Exeter range rather than the Merrimack or Rockingham groups, as many have done. I looked over the Newmarket mine, and perceived that some galena had been taken from it, apparently not a great amount. A dry looking quartz, and considerable tourmaline like that occurring in Lebanon (see p. 104, Part IV), were also observed in the opening. The Exeter range is like the Newburyport rock, but parallel with it.

THE MERRIMACK SILVER MINE, OF NEWBURYPORT.

From the reports of Prof. F. L. Vinton, made September 28, 1876, Dr. R. P. Stevens's, made April 13, 1877, and the superintendent of the mine, Edgar Shaw, I glean the following points of interest. Facts about the history of its working, change of proprietorship, etc., are irrelevant to our purpose, and will not be mentioned. The country rock is our Exeter sienite. The ores occur in a vertical fissure-lode fully 200 feet wide, traced two miles in a north-east-south-west course, but not of uniform thickness or value over this distance. The lode mass is compact trap with quartz, seams of indurated calcareous clay and selvages of softer clay, especially on the north-west wall. The ore band wrought lies near this north-west or foot-wall, and consists of argentiferous galena, accompanied by gray copper or tetrahedrite, with a gangue of quartz.

Heavy spar, fluor, pyrites, copper pyrites, and blende occur in small amount. For the depth of 60 feet, the galena constitutes a sheet averaging 12 inches wide. Below this level the ore is more crystalline; and the lode clearly discernible to the depth of 220 feet. There are five levels in the mine, and two shafts; and Prof. Vinton estimated that 40,000 gross tons of ore were actually in sight, which may be concentrated to 4,000 tons of dressed ore worth $94 per ton. The ore in sight on the first level was 1,500 cubic yards, and 10,000 upon the fifth or lowest. Underground, the vein has been explored a distance of 400 feet. The best part of the ore is situated in a chimney, nearly vertical, but inclined south-west, and averaging a width of 100 feet on the several levels.

Dr. Stevens mentions a mass of auriferous quartz parallel to the lead seam on the south-east side, varying in width from one yard at the 60-feet level to 5 feet at the 150-feet level and lower down. Working tests of the value of the quartz gave $11 of silver and $9 of gold to the ton. He also refers to the probable existence of a narrow seam of tetrahedrite continuous with the main galena belt. This mineral is exceedingly rich in silver, the maximum being $4,610.62 to the ton. The galenas average about $60 to the ton, and have been the principal resource from which bullion has been obtained.

The mine is well equipped with the necessary appliances for working, and smelting or reducing works are nearly or quite ready for use. The community have differed in opinion respecting the value of the property. It is obvious that heretofore the aim of the managers has been speculative. Most of the openings in the neighboring towns are of little value. We have the same rock in New Hampshire; and whenever indications are found similar to those manifested at Newburyport, exploration may lead to remunerative mining.

Maps of the Mining Region.

Before beginning a description of the copper mines, I will call attention to two maps. The first is a geological delineation of the Ammonoosuc mining district, and is placed for convenience in the atlas, and referred to upon page 280 in Volume II. It is designed to embrace the final results of all our topographical, geological, and economic studies, prepared for the engraver and colored at the latest possible date. The scale is about three fourths of a mile to the inch, and it is sufficiently large to show all important features. All the material at our command has been made use of, supplemented by a special survey made by Major John N. McClintock for us of the territory west of the Ammonoosuc river. The geological coloring is much the same as that on the general map, save that the representations of the auriferous conglomerate and copper belts have been added. When Volume II was written, it was not known that this band occurred east of Lisbon village. The modified drift is not distinguished.

The other map is a special survey of the Gardner Mountain copper district, prepared by J. N. McClintock. An error in the boundary line between Monroe and Lyman is my own. Contours for every ten feet are represented, and the outer edge of the wooded areas. It is designed to show the mineral proprietorship of the several tracts of land, both those valuable for ores contained, and the intervening farms. The colors show the shapes of the several tracts better than the lines alone. The following is a list of them, beginning at the north end, with their dimensions, and the nature of the minerals present:

Name.	Acres.	Mineral.
Gardner Mountain Company	250	Copper.
Kinney farm	250	Copper.
Carter farm—scattered lots	250	Copper.
Carter mine	100	Copper.
Gregory Company	160	Copper.
Wendall lot	100	Not explored.
Penhallow lot	300	Not explored.
Paddock Company	1200	Copper, lead, and silver.
Titus	250	
Richardson	250	
Abram Smith	450	
Paddock Silver Lead	300	Lead and silver.
Haviland Company	160	Copper.
Dow lot	120	Copper.
Stevens Company	160	Copper.

The map delineates the original lots of Lyman township. Farther to the south, in Bath, are three or four additional openings for copper, the

OVERSIZE FOLDOUT

(LARGER THAN 11X17)

UNABLE TO SCAN

last known as the Forsaith mine. The site of Paddock's mill is also shown.*

Copper.

The region covered by these maps will first be considered. There are at least four belts of cupreous rocks situated upon and adjacent to Gardner mountain. Including some exposures in Waterford, the distance of the remotest openings from each other is 12 miles. The richest veins follow the mountain, and have been exploited principally upon the east side. The rocks have been described heretofore as the Lisbon and Lyman divisions of the Upper Huronian, believed to correspond with the lower copper belt of Lake Superior in age. The former of these divisions consists mainly of our "greenstones" or chlorite schists, metamorphic diorites, and diabases, with dolomites. The latter or Lyman series consists mainly of argillitic schists and slates passing into quartzites. Both these formations carry copper. I do not feel confident that the distinctions between these formations are well shown through Lyman and Monroe. The principal portion of the mountain range consists of the argillitic schist, agreeing in mineral composition with the *kellas* of Cornwall. They are altered clays, containing more or less silica, sometimes passing into quartzites. The range to the east, represented by the Quint mine in Littleton, and that in Monroe, are connected with the chloritic schists and diabases. The same series, with inferior copper seams, crops out in Lisbon, underlying the village.

The same formations are developed in Quebec province about Sherbrooke, Ascot, Lennoxville, etc., where they are filled with copper veins. More openings have been made in this formation in Quebec than in Lyman. A few of the mines there have turned out well, having been operated profitably for the past twelve years. Logan referred these rocks to the altered Quebec group, a view adopted by us in our first annual report, but abandoned soon after.

The ore of copper is chalcopyrite,—the common yellow sulphuret of iron and copper,—consisting of sulphur, 34.6; copper, 34.6; iron, 30.5=

* The positions of all the known pits and openings for copper are indicated by a bright color. Upon some of the lots it is possible to observe six or seven of these openings upon veins parallel to one another. The accurate tracing out of these subordinate lines is a matter of great difficulty, and can hardly be stated with precision at present. Of the general arrangement and direction of the whole series, the map speaks plainly.

100. Excepting occasional blue and green carbonates and the black oxide, any other ores of copper are scarce in this region. The associated ores are argentiferous galena, zinc blende, and an abundance of pyrrhotite, the last named frequently forming beds by itself with slight percentages of copper. All these ores may be auriferous, but to how great an extent remains to be proved.

The veins are usually situated in broad belts of intermingled pyritiferous and siliceous layers, separated by elvans or diorites. The immediate veins may be one, two, or more feet wide, often so close together as to be practically from six to ten feet broad. The ore is in massive, not crystalline bunches, most abundant immediately contiguous to nodules of quartz. Several cases of small veins crossing the strata will be described in connection with individual mines. Our theory as to the origin of the deposits has been that they were originally beds, not fissure veins; and that in later periods the copper has been segregated from the general metalliferous belt into the several strings and veins making up the richest portions. These are found intersected by small cross veins of ore with scarcely any gangue, so that, as the country is exploited more and more, the evidences of the presence of the copper in so-called fissure-lodes increase.

I have thought the continuity of the vein is to be seen in the presence of a series of lenticular patches or bonanzas, not succeeding each other on absolutely the same plane, but overlapping. On this view, what seems to be the same vein in adjacent lots is rather a series of flattened bunches, working more and more to one side. I have not yet discovered irregularities in the veins on Gardner mountain corresponding in magnitude with those of the auriferous conglomerate in the southeast part of the town, though only exploration is needed to develop them.

I will now describe the features of the several mines in detail.

Gardner Mountain Copper Company. This property consists of 250 acres of land held in fee simple, a farm-house with the usual outbuildings, and the improvements effected for mining purposes. Much of the land has been cleared, a part remaining wooded. It has been known heretofore as the Albee mine, from its former owner, J. A. Albee. The principal outcrops are on a hill several hundred feet above the Connecticut, sloping northerly. The eastern slope is precipitous. The veins are hence well situated for exploration by cross-cuts, or through a drift following the course of the metalliferous rock. The rocks are mainly argillitic schists carrying bands of cupreous ores. There are three distinct metalliferous belts, divided by two greenstones (or sandstone, as called by the miners). Their character is indicated at the surface by yellowish-brown ferruginous stains. When these are dug into, iron or copper pyrites invariably show themselves. The most western of these belts is 178 feet wide, measuring from a point close by the shaft-house. A small opening upon this belt, several hundred feet to the south-west, shows copper. The middle belt is 87 feet wide. A shaft 78 feet deep is on its west side. It was not practicable to descend this opening at the time of my visit (October 5, 1877); but the piles of rock about the shaft-house reveal the nature of the materials brought up from the lowest depth. The vein matter is a mixture of slate and quartz, with bright yellow copper sulphuret conspicuously disseminated through it, in company with pyrites, or mundic, and a few crystals of ankerite. The ore pile contains over 100 tons, showing well in copper. It was said that the whole width of the vein had not been disclosed at the bottom of the shaft. Near the copper ore are piles of compact pyrrhotite, somewhat cupreous and perhaps auriferous, which came from the upper part of the opening. My report for 1869 made the following statement respecting this property, based upon observations upon this opening: "On Albee's land several openings have been made, in one case 20 feet deep. There seems to be a sprinkling of copper in the schist for a width of 30 feet; and near the lower edge of the cupreous rock is a solid mass of iron and copper pyrites three feet wide, the former mineral preponderating. These features are promising for a good mine. The Cornish miners prefer to see the iron pyrites or "mundic" very abundant at the surface, knowing by experience that the copper pyrites gradually takes its place according to the depth of the excavations. Our observation satisfies us that this rule holds as good in North America as in Cornwall." A gentleman who descended the shaft recently told me that the copper-bearing vein varies in width from six inches to eight feet, and the ore differs in quality from 1⅛ per cent. at the surface to 28½ per cent. at the depth of 60 feet. To the south-east of the shaft are 150 feet of metalliferous schists, belonging to the eastern belt, extending from the eastern sandstone to the edge of a precipice. Two openings showing copper ore have been made in it,—the first, 25 feet across it, and 5 or 6 in depth; the second, 6 or 7 feet long, 40 feet nearer the precipice. If these openings were connected, the whole distance would probably present the same cupreous color. These beds dip from 70°–75° S. 60°–70° E.

Since my visit, the shaft has been sunk to 70 feet depth, and a new one commenced farther east and excavated 50 feet. The company consist of energetic capitalists from Portland, Me., and they propose to sink 150 feet further in the new locality.

The Gregory Mine. This is situated in the eastern copper belt, upon a ridge 4,000 feet easterly from the Gardner Mountain mine, and separated from the former by a valley 250–300 feet deep. In 1869 I made the following statements respecting it:

"The only copper opening on the eastern belt in Littleton is at Mr. Little's, near the town line. A shaft 18½ feet deep has been sunk in the centre of a mass of copper-bearing schist 40 feet wide. The richest portion of this mass is a vein six or seven inches wide, which at the bottom of the shaft has expanded to nearly three feet in average width. The general appearance of this property reminds one of the rock worked near Lennoxville, P. Q., on what is known as the Clark mine. On the Little estate the vein must extend for 150 rods, and the surface descends rapidly to the Connecticut river, so that a fine opportunity is here presented for the excavation of an adit along the course of the vein, which will both drain the shaft above and prove the value of the rock for a considerable distance."

In September, 1877, I found the mine in possession of gentlemen from Maine, who were at work sinking the same shaft I saw in 1869. It had then reached the depth of 60 feet. Another shaft, 78 feet distant, has been sunk in the barn to the depth of 53 feet; and a drift has been started to connect them together, the space not excavated being only 16 feet. In the south shaft there is a drift northerly 25 feet at the depth of 30 feet, and 18 feet to the south at the 25-feet level. At the bottom of this shaft a breadth of two feet contains much copper associated with quartz bunches. The rest of the space in the shaft has more or less of the ore scattered throughout. Neither wall was seen, the sinking having been prosecuted with the idea of reaching as great a depth as possible, without reference to its bounds. The large pieces brought out of the south shaft make the most brilliant specimens of any seen in the range, there being very little iron pyrites to lessen the bright yellow color. Large piles of ore are found in the barn and yard. One lot of twelve tons of seven per cent. ore has been sold from the barn shaft, and much remains there dressed to about the same proportion. There is no shaft-house except the barn, but a very good boarding-house for the miners. We traced the vein northerly upon the crest of the hill, the manifestation of it there consisting of pyritiferous schists. The width of the best part of this vein is thought to be six feet; and the two walls, when seen, consist of the homogeneous "sandstone" of the country. The hoisting is done by horse-power; and there is considerable water in the mine.

During the past winter, work has been continued. A drift has been driven 30 feet into the hanging wall, in order to determine the width of the vein. Ore was found sprinkled through the whole distance.

Haviland Mine. This mine is situated on the Bath line, on the road from Lisbon to McIndoes Falls over Gardner mountain. It embraces a tract of land amounting to 160 acres, partly wooded and partly suitable for pasturage. The shaft-house is half a mile back from the highway. The argillitic schists usually dip about 70° S. 40° E. Narrow bands of diorite rock or "sandstone" are interspersed with pyritiferous schists. At the time of my visit, September 27, 1877, the shaft had been sunk 169 feet, sloping with the vein, steeper at the top than at the bottom. It is in a pyritiferous belt 200 feet wide at the surface. At 70 feet is a short drift, where copper ore is disseminated through the schist. At 168 feet the rock has been cut 40 feet below the lower wall, and 30 feet towards the hanging wall. Through this 70 feet of cutting, seams of cupriferous mundic and copper sulphurets are constantly met with. There is a marked improvement over the surface rock in what has been brought up from the lowest depths. Four veins cross this land,—one to the east, and two west from the shaft. Two or three other openings upon this land show more copper than at the shaft. This shaft has been sunk through the sandstone belt, which is 13 feet wide at 160 feet. The schists on the east are 100 feet wide before striking the next sandstone beyond, which is the most eastern copper belt.

During the winter of 1878 work has been continued, and the shaft is now down 200 feet. At the 60 feet level is a drift of 30 feet; and at the 100 feet level is another drift 40 feet long. The mine is named from F. P. Haviland, of Waterville, Me.

Stevens Mine. This lies near the north line of Bath, to the south of the Haviland. It contains 130 acres of tillage, pasturage, and woodland, and lies upon the southern slope of the Gardner mountain range. In coming from the Haviland mine the contour lines show a slight change in the direction of the mountain.. The mining improvements consist of a small boarding-house, shaft house with a shaft 100 feet deep (Sept. 26, 1877), cross cut 150 feet long at the bottom, and four other small openings in various places.

The shaft follows down a band of cupreous schists several feet wide, the angle of descent being greatest at the top. Three prominent bands of copper ore are seen at the surface, gradually widening in the descent, each one being twelve inches, and solid at the bottom. Prof. Bartlett's assay gives $37 worth of gold to the ton as coming from the pyrrhotite in these seams. There is a large pile of this ore outside of the shaft house. About 200 feet west is another vein showing copper ore along a breadth varying from two to eight feet, the gangue being white quartz with the mineral scattered through it, instead of cupreous argillitic schists, as in the first instance. This has been opened some ten or twelve feet in depth. There is a third vein about 150 feet east of the shaft, which can easily be reached underground from the main shaft. A fourth vein occurs 400 feet east of the shaft. Thus three veins are reached by one shaft less than 400 feet apart. In April, 1878, I learn that the cross cut 100 feet deep has reached the vein to the west, and ore is being raised from it. The "silver vein" is an opening on the southern slope to the west of the copper excavations. There is here a trench 25–30 feet in length, displaying a vein of galena 18 inches wide. Several barrels of this ore have been taken out. It is said to contain, of silver, $50 to the ton. It is of value in the future development of the country in connection with the argentiferous veins at the Paddock lead and copper mines. An unusual feature of the Stevens property is the occurrence of numerous boulders of copper and iron pyrites on the south slope. By reference to the maps it will appear that the main ridge of the Gardner mountain is bent to the east as it passes into Bath, and diminishes in size. It is on that southern slope that these boulders occur, noticed even twenty-five years ago. Such stones have not been observed on the eastern slope of the mountain all through Lyman. While it is possible they may have been derived from the veins to the north, the laws of boulder distribution imply their derivation from some locality near at hand, perhaps not north of the Bath line. Their occurrence recalls the discovery of the valuable mines about Capleton, P. Q., from similar indications. The presence of cupreous boulders on a similar south slope led to a search for their source, and the vein was discovered quite near at hand, and proved to be richer than any others in the district.

Paddock Company. This is the largest of all the copper companies, embracing partly in fee simple the entire land and partly the mineral rights upon four of the original lots of the town of Lyman, and therefore supposed to contain 1200 acres. The course of the veins is more than three miles in length, reaching from the Titus farm upon the south to an unoccupied tract called on our map the Penhallow lot. J. H. Paddock, Esq., of St. Johnsbury, Vt., is the principal proprietor, and the manager of the mine and mill. He has brought together several of the tracts known ten years ago as the Oro, Osgood, Osborn, New Hampshire Silver Lead Co., etc. What were formerly the Oro and Osgood openings are now the No. 1 and No. 2 shafts of the Paddock mine. Concerning these two mines, I wrote as follows in 1869:

"The next is called the Osgood mine, embracing about 700 acres of the land on the east slope of Gardner's mountain. I examined four or five openings. The first, near the south line, was ten feet deep, exhibiting five feet width of copper schists. The second shows a width of ten feet of copper schists. The third is a shaft thirty-five feet deep. Eighty feet below is a short tunnel eighty feet long, and designed to cut the vein. A large pile of good specimens of this copper may be seen near the shaft.

"The next north is the Oro mine. Here is a shaft sixty-five feet deep, a shaft house, easily seen from a great distance on account of its conspicuous position, two drifts fourteen and sixteen feet long, and a vein from four to seven feet wide, carrying more ore near the hanging than the foot wall. Sixty tons, part yielding 10.80, and part 9.+ per cent. of copper, have been shipped from the mine to Boston. There are one hundred and seventy-five acres of land connected with this property, and the vein is eighty-eight rods long."

I have visited the No. 1 shaft several times during the past nine years, watching with interest the progress indicated. Work has not been done continuously. It may be sufficient to mention the present [April, 1878] aspect of the excavation. All the laborers have been transferred to the No. 1 shaft for the purpose of developing that one more rapidly than if two were being exploited at the same time. Seven miners are at work under the superintendence of Capt. Francis Bennett, recently of the copper mines about Lenoxville, P. Q. The depth of the shaft is 170 feet. It follows the vein very nearly in its course. Extensive levels are situated at ten and twenty fathoms depth. Ore has been taken from one or both of these for a distance of 80 feet lengthwise of the vein. It has been proved that the vein is continuous for the distance of 80 feet, though not perfectly straight. There are two well-marked bendings exhibited, the arc of the curve pointing easterly, and these were seen to correspond with eastward thrusts of a dolomite band at the surface. These irregularities recall the similar varied courses of the auriferous conglomerate in the east part of the town (see map, page 296, Vol. II), though much less extensive. Without doubt the careful exploitation of Gardner's mountain in years to come will reveal bends and fractures corresponding with those in the east part of the town. There are other cross cuts in the No. 1 mine confirming the truth of the continuity oft he vein, and, by inference, its probable extent indefinitely in both directions. At present a large body of ore is in sight near the twenty fathoms level, and it is being rapidly brought to the surface. The good ore occupies a width of from four to six feet. Quite recently Capt. Bennett has discovered along the foot wall a vein of silver-lead, referred to above. This is more extensive and persistent at the twenty than at the ten fathoms level, being often ten inches in width, with the quartz gangue included. Zinc blende or black jack had been noticed before as an occasional product, but it is now found to accompany the galena, the latter increasing with the depth. The discovery is of great importance, as it may lead to the development of silver mining along the mountain. The copper vein is composed of grayish-white quartz, much harder than the greenish schists adjacent. Similar veins occur in the other mining properties on the range, some of which may be the continuation of this. The map shows at least six parallel veins upon this property. One is characterized by the grayish-white quartz present; another exhibits more of a slaty aspect, as at No. 2; a third is a mass of pyrrhotite. The others are intermediate in character between the first two mentioned. The third is known as the mundic vein, and has been followed for more than a mile along the east foot of the mountains. It is slightly cupreous, and may prove to be richly so at a considerable depth, if it resembles similar veins in other metalliferous districts. The amount of ore produced from the No. 1 shaft previous to 1874 is thought to have amounted to 300 tons. Much more than that has been taken out since; but I understand the aim has been to develop the mine, to learn the extent of the veins, rather than to raise a large amount of ore. A road has been built to connect both the shafts with the mill, a mile and a half distant.

At the No. 2 shaft the adit is now 90 feet long, and the veins at the surface overhead have been extensively uncovered. A most interesting feature is the existence of a small cross vein, cutting the strata two feet wide where thickest, and uncovered for eighty feet up the mountain. It contains more copper than the regular vein. Possibly it may extend to join a vein about 170 feet further up the mountain, and but slightly exploited. This and the galena vein on top of the mountain are the only cross veins yet discovered, but as time progresses others will be discovered much larger and more important than these. From these, we may conclude that these copper beds are properly fissure lodes, though so commonly conformable to the stratification, and therefore more highly esteemed. At one visit I saw about 150 tons of dressed ore near the mouth of the adit thought to average 6 per cent. of copper present. It was found that this ore would roast much more quickly than that occurring in the Vermont mines, as at Vershire and Strafford. They differ also in containing an excess of silica rather than iron. For similar reasons, one accustomed to estimate the percentage of copper in the Vermont ores will be inclined to undervalue the worth of the New Hampshire product.

Concentration of Ores. It may be well to anticipate the proper order of description, and mention the contrivances employed by Mr. Paddock to reduce the bulk of the copper ores while increasing their value. It is of no use to send to market lean ores, because of the expense of transporting worthless rock. Hence various methods are in use to concentrate them. The oldest method is to pick out the best pieces and throw away the poorer ones. In this way these ores may be easily brought to 8 or 10 per cent. valuation. When the metal is very abundant, another process reduces the ores in a furnace by smelting to a matt of 40 or 60 per cent. copper, and thus saves a great deal in transportation. Another method, well adapted to the New Hampshire ore, is to remove the copper by a wet process of extraction. This will be mentioned soon in detail. Still another plan has been adopted by Mr. Paddock. The ore is pulverized, and the copper ore separated from the lighter worthless rock by virtue of its greater weight. Wet and dry jigs are used for this purpose, and the results appear to be satisfactory. The ores are concentrated to 15 or 20 per cent. in this way, very cheaply, and are in excellent condition for smelting.

To carry on this business a mill is required, estimated to cost, with all the apparatus, if set up new, about $17,000. There must be an engine, a crusher, apparatus for elevating the crushed rock to an upper chamber where sieves may classify the material into several sizes, and the dry and wet jigs. I will briefly describe the process as it is being carried on at the mill in Lyman. An engine is at work driving a rock-crusher, elevating the powdered rock, shaking both jigs, drying the wet products, and for other purposes. It requires the services of one person to keep the engine in order, and a second to furnish rock for the crusher. In the upper chamber are sieves separating the pulverized rock into five parts; first, the coarser pieces, which are made automatically to descend to the wet jig in the basement; second, three grades of coarseness, suitable for the Chubb concentrator, or dry jig; lastly, the slums or dust, which is too fine to be separated by either of the jigs. No attendance is required to separate these different grades and carry them to their proper places; the business is attended to by machinery. The Chubb separator is a patented contrivance, making use of intermittent air puffs to classify the material into three parts; first, the ore concentrated to its utmost extent; second, the worthless material fit only to be thrown away; and third, the middlings, a mixture of the other two kinds, which is made to go through the machine a second time. Without technical description, this apparatus may be styled a trough about 4 by 2 feet, placed over a bellows blowing 300 to 500 times a minute, according to circumstances. The air is forced through a perforated metallic plate, and the box is at the same time skaken. By these means the pulverized ore is separated into the three kinds of powder mentioned, according to relative weight, and gradually slides to the lower part of the boxes, the separation being facilitated by a slight inclination and the presence of diagonal partitions of metal strips. An attendant watches the delivery of the product into boxes, properly separating the three kinds with the assistance of movable partitions. One person can easily attend to the three machines employed in the mill, and perhaps as many as five. It is his business also to remove the boxes receiving the finished products as often as necessary, put the ore into the barrels provided for it, the refuse into its place, and the middlings back into hoppers. Meanwhile, another person in the basement watches the wet jig, where large sieves filled with the coarser rock are jigged underneath water, and the heavier parts sink to the bottom. In a short time the worthless material is thrown away, the heaviest put upon a steam-heated table and dried, preliminary to package in barrels for transportation, and the middlings saved for another washing. I have examined the tailings left from both kinds of jigs, and observe that scarcely any ore escapes. Both processes separate the ore very carefully, and the waste is only slight. One grade of the ore remains,—the dust or slums. At present this is preserved for experiment, as the best method of saving the copper ore in it has not been perfected. Tossing in water is recommended, and will perhaps be the most convenient method of separation. It seems to me that a wet chemical process might be used to good advantage, such as will be described presently.

I have been greatly pleased with the results obtained practically by this mill, and think that the processes employed will enable our mining companies to utilize their poorer ores to better advantage than before. I understand that the Chubb patent embodies peculiarities not existing in any other separator, and is better adapted than any other machine for this class of ore. It has been in use many months in Lyman, and has successfully treated as much as 100 or 200 tons of ore, so that its value has been well tested. In case it should be taken for new localities, it is recommended that it be placed at the mouth of the mine, and thus save any unnecessary transportation of the ore before concentration, and the steam-power could also be utilized for hoisting purposes.

Quint Mine. A mile or two east of the Gregory is the Quint or White Mountain copper mine, in Littleton. No copper property in this region had been so thoroughly explored as this in 1869; several buildings have been erected for shaft-house, whim, dressing-sheds, etc., and the main shaft has been sunk to the depth of one hundred feet. It was impossible for me to examine the character of the rock below the surface, as all the excavations were filled with water; but, judging from external appearances, the vein must be from six to eight feet wide, composed of white quartz with copper sulphuret, iron pyrites, chlorite, and ankerite disseminated abundantly through it. On account of the contrast in colors, very beautiful hand specimens may be obtained here. The location is a poor one, so far as drainage is concerned.

Other Properties. There are many other farms where copper has been found, and, in some cases, extensively opened. There were three examined north of the No. 1 shaft of the Paddock company in 1869, known as the Stevens and Nason, Locke, Swan and Garland, and now belonging to Mr. Paddock. All of them showed excavations a few feet in depth, a mixture of the usual iron and copper pyrites in the schists several feet wide.

Dr. Jackson examined copper upon Lang's property in Bath, adjoining the Stevens mine. From his reports I condense the following facts: Two veins occur crossing at right angles, north-east and north-west courses. One of them is from one foot to eighteen inches wide, the other thicker. A detached block of pure ore, two and a half feet in diameter, was found in the meadow. A single blast afforded 100 pounds of 20 per cent. ore.

Farther south, as shown on the map, are three other copper locations. The most southern on the crest of the mountain is called the Forsaith mine, containing 140 acres, showing quite a number of small openings, all of them showing copper ore.

There are several openings in Monroe, on the west side of Gardner's mountain. I have presumed the copper belt is repeated here, and the cupreous schists occur in many places, though comparatively little work has been done. The largest opening is upon the Bald ledge, operated several years since by Mr. Paddock. The best part of the copper schist is six feet wide, containing, in addition to the usual minerals, zinc blende and obliquely crossing veins of quartz. The shaft-house is very high up, so that the vein could be well drained to a considerable depth. The shaft was sunk to the depth of 80 feet. Ten tons of 10 per cent. ore were the result of this exploitation. Farther west, down the hill, is another vein, possibly connected synclinally with the ore high up.

In Littleton and Dalton are two openings, showing the purple and gray ores of copper. One is on Wheeler hill, and the other is known as the Dalton mine, where work has been performed under the direction of J. B. Sumner, Esq. The rock of the country is clay slate, but the gangue of the vein is a species of talcose schist, containing a little yellow copper and minute particles of magnetic iron. The walls of the Dalton mine are very distinct, about sixteen feet apart. The gangue is traversed by cross veins of quartz, often carrying fine specimens of the purple ore, or *Bornite*. A shaft has been sunk about twenty-five feet deep upon the vein, and a few openings have been made as far as 200 or 300 feet north of the shaft-house, sufficiently to prove the continuation of the vein. Similar proof exists of the presence of copper, perhaps the same vein, half a mile in the other direction. This property is upon the top of a hill. It is conveniently situated with reference to water-power, being near the Connecticut and one of its tributaries, so that the ore taken from the mine could very easily be concentrated at slight expense. An average sample of the whole vein sent by Mr. Sumner gave to Prof. Seely 5.4 per cent. of metallic copper.

Copper in Milan. Similar ores to those of Gardner mountain have been discovered lately in Milan. The formation is the same. I have examined several openings. First is that of Nathan Fogg, a short distance east of the Grand Trunk Railway. The vein dips 70° N. W. A pit has been sunk in it about fifteen feet, close by a small brook, and the ore shows well for a width of thirteen feet. It is a massive mixture of copper and iron pyrites, with galena and blende, without much gangue. A fair average gave C. W. Kempton 5.3 per cent. of copper. Immediately adjacent to the foot wall is a pretty string of argentiferous galena, half an inch wide. The upper part of the vein also shows much galena and bright bunches of copper. An assay of the average under my supervision yielded a trace of gold and 2.65 ounces of silver to the ton. Excavations prove the continuation of the vein for at least 200 feet, and in one place there is a width of 40 feet of pyritiferous schists connected with the vein. The situation is very convenient to railroad transportation.

On the hill west, Mr. Nay has opened a seam running north-west, though tending to take the north-east course of the strata, which contains argentiferous galena. Mr. Nay has uncovered the rock in several places, but had not proved the value of the property at the time of my visit in August, 1877.

On Hodgdon's land, to the north, is the Twitchell and Mason mine.

They have cut into pyritiferous schists, sinking upon a vein six feet wide, richer than the usual mass of 40 feet thickness. Many bunches of copper were taken out, and I understand from F. L. Bartlett, of Portland, that nickel is present in the ore.

On Cate's hill, in Berlin, is a vein showing the minerals pyrite, chalcopyrite, bornite, magnetite, hornblende, and tremolite. The ores are sparsely disseminated.

This region promises well to the explorer, and it will doubtless be heard from in the future. Our map shows that the rocks continue here from the Ammonoosuc district, though interrupted by intrusive porphyries.

THE WARREN MINE.

In the gneiss of Warren there is a bed of tremolite more than fifty feet wide, in connection with which is a vein of copper and zinc. Mica schist, dipping 45° N. 50° E., encloses the bed. Veins of pure copper ore with reticulations of quartz abound in the hanging wall, and a bed of the same material occurs along the line of the junction of the tremolite and schist. Veins of the copper, bunches of iron pyrites, and a resplendent black blende occur also in the midst of the tremolite, as well as a little rutile. Most of the tremolite carries copper pyrites, and the rock must be stamped and washed to allow of separation. The annexed plan shows

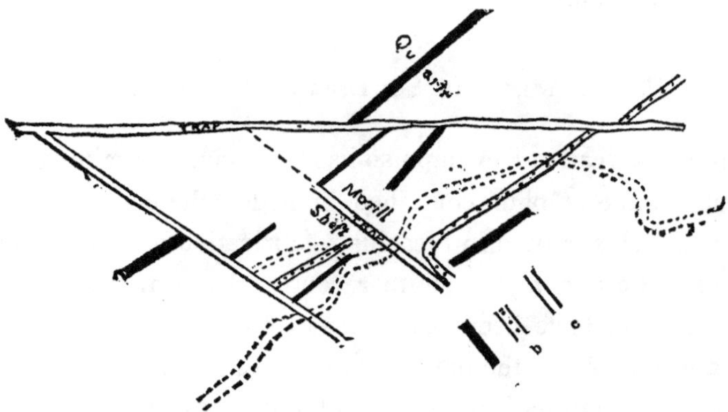

Fig. 7.—PLAN OF THE WARREN MINE.

a, Quartz; b, Ore vein; c, Trap.

the mutual relations of the three trap dykes, veins of quartz, and the ore vein. It was prepared by Mr. Huntington, and is not drawn to a scale.

Considerable work has been done upon this property since 1840. The tremolite does not occur with the copper at great depths. Latterly the zinc predominates, and there is a little galena. At the time of my visit the mine was full of water, and I could learn little in addition to what has been presented. I made the following statements respecting it in 1869:

The Warren zinc mine is now under the management of Capt. Edgar. It has been known for twenty years as a copper mine, but as the vein has been followed downwards the zinc has to a considerable extent increased at the expense of the copper, and it is for the zinc chiefly that the mine is now wrought. The principal vein is of quartz, ten feet wide, crossed by a mass of the mineral tremolite. The hanging wall is a sandstone, the foot wall micaceous slate. To the depth of twenty-five feet, copper ore and galena predominated. Below that point, to the bottom of the excavation, one hundred and fifty feet, the zinc is the most abundant, amounting to one half. At the bottom the vein is twenty feet wide, and there is a drift one hundred and eighty feet in length. There seems to be a "pipe" or "chimney" of pure ore in the vein, sometimes fifteen feet thick and twenty broad, which is the most valuable part of the metallic sheet. It does not proceed on the direct line of the dip, but passes down about ten degrees from it.

At present (1869) the ore is first sent to the Lowell Bleachery Company, Mass., where the sulphur is removed and converted into sulphuric acid. The residue then goes to Bethlehem, Pa., where it is smelted into spelter.

Since 1870 the mine has not been worked. It is owned by Horace Brooks, of Franconia.

Copper Mines in Southern New Hampshire.

Within a few years a new impulse has been given to mining for pyrites, on account of the sulphur contained in it, for the manufacture of sulphuric acid. This is used in bleaching, fabrication of artificial fertilizers, and a hundred other ways. Quite recently, chemical works for the utilization of sulphur have been established about the principal cities, and there is a great call for the ores containing sulphur. By the burning of the ore,—a sulphuret of iron,—the sulphur takes oxygen from the air, becoming sulphurous acid. This is condensed in water in leaden chambers, where an additional atom of oxygen is added, and the resulting compound is sulphuric acid. One of the principal sources of this pyrites is Strafford, Vt., where copperas has been manufactured for the past fifty years. From that single locality on Copperas hill, thousands of tons of ore have been sent to market. The species is pyrrhotite, containing 39.5 per cent. of sulphur, and is therefore less valuable than common pyrites, which has 53.3 per cent. of sulphur.

There are several veins of pyrites in New Hampshire that can be successfully mined for the manufacturing establishments, especially as copper is usually associated with them. These veins are also nearer the market than those of Vermont, which are now mined so largely. Perhaps the most important of these is in the south-west part of Croydon. This has been visited twice,—in June, 1869, and May, 1870. The results of our examination are briefly these: The rock is micaceous and gneissic, one of the sub-divisions of the White Mountain series probably. It is elevated two or three hundred feet, on the south-east flank of Croydon mountain. Higher up is the quartzite, dipping at a high angle to N. 65° W. It probably overlies the sulphuret schist unconformably, as it certainly does three miles farther north, the latter dipping 80° W. 10° S. One or two hundred feet east of the vein is a white gneissic rock, carrying an unusual amount of mica. This is parallel with it, and may be used as a guide in tracing it through the country. In this way the vein was followed for three fourths of a mile to the north, and from what was said to us, it is judged to extend equally far to the south. The vein has been opened to the depth of twenty-five feet. It was full of water at our first visit, but was drained at the second visit by means of a syphon. The vein mass is uniform in its width and composition. Next the hanging wall is six inches width of slaty layers, holding both copper and iron pyrites. Next succeeds two feet thickness of magnetic pyrites, or pyrrhotite, very compact, solid, and nearly pure. There is no foreign mineral present except small nodules of quartz. Next follows one foot ten inches of the same, less compact. Fourthly, is two feet thickness of gangue of quartz, or a micaceous mass carrying a large proportion of copper pyrites and zincblende. Below all this is a slaty mass three or four feet in thickness, similar to the upper layer, carrying considerable pyrites, which possibly may be utilized. The second, third, and fourth of these layers are valuable, and united amount to six feet in thickness. By Prof. Seely's determination, the sulphur in No. 2 amounts to 37.68

per cent.; in No. 3, to 38.10 per cent.; and in No. 4, to 19.35 per cent. No. 4 also contains 3.17 of copper and 16.62 per cent. of zinc.

On examining the veins to the north the sulphurets are found cropping out on the surface for one or two hundred feet, and the vein itself can be traced on the property nearly to a house eighty rods distant. Further tracing was not attempted in that direction. It is common for this vein to be cut by irregular veins of white quartz.

The outcrops are on a steep hill, perhaps three hundred feet above a comparatively level tract. Thus the vein could be easily drained, whether an adit be driven into the hill at right angles to the vein, or from the north and driven in on the vein itself. This site is less than three miles in a gently ascending country from Northville (Newport), on the Concord & Claremont Railroad.

Neal Mine. Next in value is the Neal mine in Unity. This has been visited three times. It is owned by the Neal family, and is about four miles from North Charlestown. The vein has been described in Dr. Jackson's report. It is a mixture of iron and copper pyrites, nearly three feet wide, and has been traced fully 2,200 feet in length. Drainage can be effected to the depth of seventy feet. The vein dips 78° W. 10° N. It has the same geological position with the Croydon mine, lying near the western border of the gneiss, and if the ores were mixed it would be difficult to distinguish many of the varieties from each other. It is probable that the ore would all become copper pyrites at 100 feet or more below the surface.

There are other interesting veins on this property, but it is only sufficient for our present purpose to say that the pyrites can be as profitably mined for sulphur here as at Croydon, and if copper or other valuable metals should be ultimately discovered in abundance, it might be wrought for them also.

Other veins carrying considerable amounts of pyrites, which are all worthy of exploration with the hope of successful results, are the King property, upon C. Houston's land, in the south-east part of Hanover; the land of J. W. Cleaveland, of East Lebanon, in the north-west part of Enfield; in the south-west part of Lebanon; Dr. Hubbard's mine on the Jackson farm, in the south part of Claremont. On account of the great value of this ore in the manufacture of fertilizers, it is to be hoped that these veins will be thoroughly explored, the market well supplied with sulphuric acid, and thus both the mining district be benefited and the prices of the phosphates be reduced, and the whole community reap the advantages of lower prices of fertilizers.

The Hunt and Douglass Process.

Other localities of copper are numerous, especially in the Connecticut valley, as in Haverhill, Orford, and Lyme. These and others are mentioned in the catalogue of mineral localities in Part IV. Some of them may prove valuable as mines after exploitation, especially one on the west flank of the hill between Mts. Cuba and Smart.

Copper is reduced at West Fairlee, Vt., by smelting. The ores of eastern Vermont and those in New Hampshire south of Woodsville, belong to a different formation from those mentioned in the Ammonoosuc district,—the Coös instead of the Huronian. Some authors, especially the managers of mining companies, inform the public of their identity. But an examination of the rocks associated with the two will show that our copper veins belong to at least three distinct periods. Our ores are usually low grade, and hence can be easily reduced by a wet process cheaper than by smelting. Having investigated the merits of the Hunt and Douglass process, I think it one well fitted to reduce our ores, and herewith present a brief notice of it, compiled from an authoritative sketch in the *Mineral Resources west of the Rocky Mountains*, for 1876:

This is what is technically called a wet method, because the copper is removed from its ores in a dissolved state, the solvent employed in the present process being a watery solution of neutral proto-chloride of iron and common salt. Most oxidized compounds of copper,—whether obtained artificially by roasting sulphuretted ores, or found in nature in the form of carbonates and oxides,—when digested with such a solution are converted into a mixture of proto-chloride of copper, which are dissolved, while the iron of the solvent separates in the form of insoluble hydrous peroxide of iron. When the solution of chlorides of copper thus obtained is brought in contact with metallic iron, the copper is separated in a metallic crystalline state, while the iron passes into solution, reproducing the proto-chloride of iron, thus restoring its solvent powers to the liquid, which we shall call "the bath," and fitting it for the treatment of a fresh portion of copper ore. This process of solution and precipitation can, under proper conditions, be repeated indefinitely with the same bath, the only reagent consumed being the metallic iron.

The chief advantages which wet processes possess over smelting lies in the economy of fuel. To extract copper from a low grade ore by smelting, five or six furnace operations are necessary, and about one ton of coal is consumed for each ton of ore treated; while for the various wet processes, a single calcination, in which not more than 300 weight of coal is consumed for each ton of ore, is the only furnace operation required to obtain the metallic copper in a precipitated form known as *cement copper*. An important item of cost in wet processes is the metallic iron employed to separate the metallic copper from its solutions. The same amount of iron is required to precipitate a ton of copper, whether extracted from a poor or a rich ore; but as for the smelting of the latter much less fuel is required, it follows that rich ores are generally treated by smelting rather than in the wet way, any saving of fuel in the latter being more than compensated for by the cost of iron. No general rule, however, can be laid down to determine what grade of ore can be more profitably treated by one method or the other, inasmuch as circumstances of locality, affecting the cost of fuel and the price of iron, must in each case be taken into account.

The various other wet methods of copper extraction may be divided into two classes: those in which the previously oxidized ore is treated with hydrochloric or sulphuric acid to dissolve the oxide of copper, and those in which sulphuretted ore, generally after a preliminary roasting, is calcined with an admixture of sea-salt or sulphate of soda, by which the copper is converted into chloride or into sulphate. All of these methods, when properly applied, effect a pretty thorough extraction of the copper; but the cost of the reagents which have to be added to every charge of ore precludes altogether the use of some of these methods, except in certain favored localities, and renders them in almost all cases, it is believed, less economical than the present one with the Hunt and Douglass bath, for which the following advantages are claimed:

I. It is a general method adapted to all compounds of copper, while that by calcination with salt is only applicable to sulphuretted ores.

II. It does not require the addition of reagents, such as acids, salt, or sulphate of soda, to each charge of ore, since in the regular course of the operation the solvent required for the treatment of the ore is constantly reproduced.

III. The bath employed being neutral, certain impurities of the ores, such as arsenic, which passes into solution and contaminates the product in the wet processes, remain undissolved, so that a purer copper is obtained.

IV. There is no unnecessary waste or consumption of metallic iron.

Ores reached by this process. First, may be included the various sulphuretted ores, as copper pyrites (often mixed with iron pyrites) and the variegated and vitreous sulphurets, all of which are readily oxidized by calcination. Second, are the oxidized compounds of copper, such as the red and black oxides, the green and blue carbonates, and salts, like the oxy-chloride and silicates like chrysocolla. Third, are the deposits of native or metallic copper, which in almost all instances are most advantageously treated by mechanical means. The presence of carbonate of lime or magnesia is objectionable, since it decomposes the proto-chloride of copper, and thus indirectly precipitates the iron from the bath. The action of oxides of lead and zinc, which come from the roasting of blende and galena when these are present in the ore, produces a similar effect. When not too abundant, the effect of all these substances may be corrected by careful roasting.

Practical workings. This process was first worked continuously for a year at the Davidson mine in North Carolina. The ore, a pyritous copper in a slaty gangue, was dressed up to 5 or 6 per cent., crushed, roasted so as to contain about one fourth of its copper as sulphate, and treated in stirring-vats in charges of 3,000 pounds. The loss of copper was from .3 to .5 per cent.; and the bath maintained its strength in chloride of iron without the use of copperas or sulphurous acid. The amount of iron consumed was equal to 70 per cent., and the salt to 25 per cent., of the copper produced. The entire cost of producing cement copper from the dressed ore of 5½ per cent. was estimated at 3⅜ cents per pound.

Next, six calcining furnaces for the treatment of twelve tons of pryitous ore daily were erected by the same proprietors at the Ore Knob mine in the same state. Up to January 1, 1875, over 200 tons of copper had been made there by this process. The cost of mining, making the copper, and all expenses, amounted to 8 cents per pound. These works were soon after enlarged to nearly three times their former capacity; but, in sinking below the water-line in the mine, the ore, hitherto free from lime, was found to contain 30 per cent. of carbonate of lime. This rendered it necessary to concentrate the ore by crushing and washing,—works for which have been erected.

At Phenixville, Penn., two sorts of copper ores are being treated by this process,—the one a magnetic iron containing about 3 per cent. of copper, the other a hydrated silicate. One ton of the first and four fifths of a ton of the second are now daily successfully treated at this locality.

The cost of the *plant*, or buildings and machinery required for the working of the process, is from $12,000 to $15,000. The details are given in the annexed letter from Dr. Hunt:

Letter from Dr. Hunt.

As you desired, I write you some notes as to our copper process, its cost and its advantages, compared with smelting or shipping ores, considered from the point of view of New Hampshire copper mines. I give, first, the cost of treating in a small work 12 tons of 2,000 pounds daily, and suppose the ore to yield 8 per cent. of copper, labor to be $1.25 a day, and wood $4 a cord:

For grinding (steam power), 1½ cords, . . .	$6.00
Labor of 3 men, at $1.25, ...	3.75
For roasting, 4 cords, ...	16.00
Labor of 12 men, ...	15.00
Tank-house, 2 men, ...	2.50
Superintendent and chemist, ...	5.00
Scrap-iron, 1,300 pounds, at 1½ cents, . .	19.60
Three hundred pounds salt, and sundries, .	4.25
	$72.00=$6 for 2,000 lbs. ore.

The cost of plant for the above, including a 32-horse-power engine, 4 furnaces, 21 tanks, and 2 pairs of rolls and buildings, has been, at Phenixville, $12,000.

To compare the above with shipping ore from Strafford to Boston. Let us suppose hauling and handling to station, $2; freight on railroad, $4.40=$6.40 per ton (the smelter's ton is 2,352 pounds). The wet assay of the ore is 8 3-10 per cent. copper, from which he deducts, according to custom, 1 3-10 cents, leaving 7 per cent. to be paid for at the present rates of $3.75 per unit.

10 gross or smelters' tons (23,520 pounds) of 7 per cent. ore at the above price will bring	$262.50	
Deduct for freight at $6.40 per ton, ...	64.00*	
		———$198.50

The above amount of ore equals 11¾ net tons of ore at 8 3-10 per cent., in treating which in the moist way the loss will not be over 5-10 per cent., leaving 7 8-10 per cent. of copper to be accounted for, or 1,833 pounds. This, as cement copper, will sell for 21 cents when ore brings $3.75 per unit, equal to $384.93. But the treatment of the ore, as we have seen above, costs $6 the ton=$70.50, to which, for packages and freight to Boston, we may add $7=$77.50.

Deducting this from $384.93, we have for net return from the ore treated by the Hunt & Douglass process, ...	$307.45	
For the ore shipped as above, ...	198.40	
		———$109.50*

To this we must add the consideration that the selection of ores of 8 3-10 per cent. for shipment involves a considerable loss, and that with rocks on the spot it would be advantageous to treat ores of much lower grade got with less labor in dressing. Deducting from the estimate above the cost of iron, which varies with the richness of the ore, we have for 12 tons $52.50=$4.38 the ton.

Suppose, then, we treat 20 tons of 5½ per cent. ore, to yield 1 ton (2,000 pounds) of copper, we have ($4.38 × 20) . . .	$87.60	
Two thirds ton scrap-iron, at 1½ cents a pound, ...	20.00	
		———$107.60

Thus the cost of producing 1 ton of copper from these low grade ores is only $107.60, while such ore would perhaps hardly pay the cost of shipping.

I have stated the principal points of interest to you, but have not referred to the use of tin plate scrap, which in most localities can be got for little or nothing, and thus save the cost of the scrap-iron, and materially reduce the cost of making copper. Our works here are not yet in full operation, but will be in the course of ten days. I shall

---

* I am told that the railways count but 2,000 pounds to the ton, so that the ten gross tons of ore would pay freight as 11⅛ tons, making freight $75.20, or $11.20 more than above, which sum must be deducted from $198.20 and added to $109, making the daily balance in favor of the Hunt & Douglass process $120.

be glad to hear from you further in this matter, and shall spend here the rest of the month.

Very truly yours, T. STERRY HUNT.

Phenixville, Pa., June 12, 1875.

Iron.

There are several localities where an abundant supply of this ore exists. At Franconia the ore was smelted for sixty years; and the iron manufactured is more highly prized than that made in other states. The remoteness of our state from the coal fields, and the decimation of our forests whereby the yield of charcoal has fallen off, have led to the abandonment of iron mining at Franconia.

The vein is of magnetic iron, associated with hornblende, epidote, garnet, mispickel, and other minerals. It is stated by Jackson to be from 3½ to 4 feet wide. It has been opened for several hundred feet on the steep south slope of Ore hill in Lisbon, and hence is unnecessarily exposed to accumulate rain-water. A shaft is situated low down, said to be 150 feet deep. At the upper end of the cut there is a curve in the vein, amounting practically to a bonanza, beyond which the direction taken by the vein is uncertain. A short adit on the west side of the hill beyond did not discover the vein, as was expected. The vein dips 70° S. 40° E. The rock on the west side of the vein is hornblende schist and gneiss.

Furnaces were erected for the manufacture of iron here in 1811, and continued in blast till 1870. Charcoal was the fuel employed. Dr. Jackson has given a full account of the special process of the manufacture of the iron, to which those interested are referred. It seems that the annual yield varied from 250 to 500 tons of pig iron, of which a part was reduced to wrought iron in a forge. The following figures expressed the cost of manufacture:

The proportions used in charging the blast furnace were 15 bushels of charcoal, 5 boxes each containing 56 pounds of magnetic ore, one box of limestone for flux. The average daily product was 2½ tons of pig. From 200,000 to 300,000 bushels of charcoal were annually consumed, taking 160 bushels for each ton of iron made. Hard wood charcoal cost $4 per hundred bushels, spruce or soft-wood charcoal, $2.50 per hundred. The limestone cost $1 per ton. The ore cost $6 per ton at the furnace at Franconia village, two or three miles distant from the mine. The items were these: mining, $5;

hauling, $0.50; breaking, $0.50. The average product of cast-iron was 60 per cent. on the ore smelted, being a loss of 9 per cent. Jackson's assay was the following: magnetic oxide, 96.20, silica, 2.30, titanic acid, 1.50=100. Metallic iron, 69.04. Ten miners were employed at the rate of $15 per month. The pig sold in 1840 at the furnace for 2 cts. per lb., castings at 5 cts. per lb., and bar iron at 5½ cts. At the furnace 100 laborers were employed for six months, and half of them for the balance of the year. The furnace buildings and the miners' houses are still standing. From a detailed statement of the superintendent, the operations for 1838 showed an expenditure of $14,128.63; sale of pig and scrap, $14,594.98; sale of castings $7,309.12,—total, $21,904.10. Excess of receipts over expenditures, $7,775.47.

At the present day the mining could be effected more cheaply than in 1840. A miner living at Sugar Hill assured me of his ability to contract for the delivery of ore at the surface for $2 per ton, provided means were taken to drain the excavation. His plan was to open the vein so low down that the water would make no trouble.

Dr. Jackson mentions two other places in the state where the natural facilities for the manufacture of iron are as good as those at Lisbon, viz., at Bartlett and Piermont. The following sketch of the Bartlett locality is furnished by Mr. Huntington. The other statement is by a friend, who is well qualified to judge of the value of ore deposits.

Iron Ore in Bartlett.

A little south of west from the village of Jackson there is a high mountain ridge, the eastern extremity of which is known as Baldface. This ridge extends to the western slope of Mt. Crawford, but it is cut by the valley of Rocky Branch, and also by a stream, Razor Branch, in the western part of Bartlett. This ridge, for the most part, is a coarse granite, composed chiefly of feldspar and quartz, but it contains some mica, and generally manganese. In this granitic rock, in the northern part of the town of Bartlett and east of Rocky Branch, occurs the most extensive deposit of workable iron ore ever found in New Hampshire.

In the ridges that project south from the ridge just mentioned the granite is of a different texture, being more compact, and the feldspar, instead of being a light flesh-color, is a dull gray, and more distinctly crystalline. This rock forms the precipitous cliffs north of the road running from Jackson to Upper Bartlett. North of the granite containing the iron and forming the mountain south of the settlement in Jackson known as Green hill, the rock is a mica schist which passes into a quartzite. The schist dips N. 40° W. at an angle of 25°, and hence it rests upon the granite. On the eastern slope of the mountain is a schist entirely different from that which forms the mass of the mountains; and besides, it has an easterly dip, and it seems probable that it is the remnant of a synclinal axis that once filled the valley of Ellis river.

This deposit of iron has been known for many years, and was first noticed by Mr. Meserve. It was visited by Dr. Jackson, and is thus described by him:

"One of the veins at the upper opening measures thirty-seven feet in width in an east and west, and sixteen in a north and south direction. The second opening, two hundred feet lower down the slope of the hill, exposes the ore, maintaining the same width. Three hundred feet lower down the vein is observed to narrow, and is but ten feet wide, and four hundred feet farther down the width increases to fifty-five feet. Five hundred and forty-six feet lower still there is a small opening or cave twenty feet deep, where the ore narrows again. On searching to the westward of this great vein, at a distance of two hundred and fifty feet, we soon discovered a new one, which appears to be of the largest dimensions. * * * Forty-nine feet farther westward the soil is full of angular fragments of the ore, indicating another vein. It is evident that this mountain is intersected by a great number of veins of excellent iron ore, and will furnish an inexhaustible supply. It is proper here to remark, that it is composed chiefly of the peroxide of iron, combined with a small proportion of the protoxide, and it contains a little oxide of manganese. From the composition of the ore we know that it will make excellent iron and the best kind of steel."

Fifty tons of the ore were sent to Sampson & Co., celebrated English iron and steel manufacturers, who have reported favorably upon its good qualities. In my examination of this ore deposit, the measurements for mapping the property were made by Daniel Barker, Esq., of Bangor, Me. Starting from the most westerly outcrop on the slope towards Rocky Branch, we found the principal outcrops to lie in a direct line running N. 42° E., and the entire distance one hundred and seventy-five rods. The last outcrop on the east is six feet in width. Measurements of the openings on the west slope towards Rocky Branch were made by Dr. Jackson when the mine was first opened, and could be done much more exact than now. In several places, particularly north of the line followed, there are indications of iron, which may prove as extensive as the beds already opened.

An analysis of the iron ore by Mr. Williams is as follows:

Peroxide of iron,	69.4
Quartz and feldspar,	25.2
Oxide of manganese,	2.7

69.4 of peroxide, containing 48.117 per cent. of metallic iron.

Another specimen yielded,—

Peroxide and protoxide of iron,	77.25
Quartz and feldspar,	21.40
Alumina,	.15
Manganese,	1.20

Or 53 per cent. of metallic iron.

The masses of ore seem to be in vertical segregations. Consequently there is more uncertainty as to their extending to a great depth, than if the ore occurred in lodes in a stratified rock; but this uncertainty is in a measure counterbalanced by the large masses in which the ore here occurs.

Until recently this ore has been far from any means of transportation by railway; but now the Portland & Ogdensburg Railroad, which extends through Bartlett, will pass within three miles of the mine, and a branch road can be easily built up Rocky Branch to a point where a tramway can be constructed to the shaft, and thus the ore can be moved altogether by steam.

The following may be considered a fair estimate as to cost of mining and profits:

200 tons of ore per day, at $2.64 per ton,	$528.00
General expense,	50.00
Freight to Portland,	300.00
Entire cost,	$878.00
Value of ore at $6 per ton,	$1,200.00

which leaves a margin of $322 per day as profit on a capital not exceeding $160,000.

The following is an estimate for a day, provided the ore is smelted in the valley of Rocky Branch near the mine:

200 tons of ore, at $2.64 per ton,	$528.00
16,000 bushels of charcoal, at 8 cents per bushel,	1,280.00
30 furnace men, at $3.50 per day,	70.00
160 laborers, at $1.50 per day,	240.00
Limestone for flux,	100.00
Repairs, etc.,	40.00
General expenses,	250.00
Freight on 100 tons of iron to Portland,	170.00
	$2,678.00

These figures, at the present (1871) price of pig iron, would leave a very large margin for profit, although the necessary outlay for the construction of furnaces, etc., would greatly increase the capital stock to be employed in carrying on the operations. The ore could probably be extracted, especially if it is done by open mining, at a much less cost than we have given in the above estimate, the location being favorable for this kind of excavation. The mine is owned by E. S. Coe & Co., of Bangor, Me.

The other statement is as follows, in a letter penned after two days of examination, dated November, 1873.

There is really iron upon Iron mountain, and some of the ore of excellent percentage; but it occurs the most capriciously of any iron I have ever come across, and the workings have not as yet revealed any reliable body of ore. In one of the little drifts, out of which apparently the greatest part of the rich ore has been taken, the rock seems barren on the right hand, and on the left, before you, and, strangest of all, under your feet. There is no vein; and yet, while the ore occurred pocket-like, it does not lie segregated in any wise from the containing rock, but passes into it on every side by imperceptible gradations. Appearances at some spots suggested the idea that the common rock of the mountain had been impregnated by the vapor of metallic iron rising from below at points where fissures and seams in the country rock permitted it. If this theory be correct, while there must be a large body of iron somewhere down below, all the ore anywhere near the surface would be in chimneys of entirely capricious distribution.

Piermont. On the road from Haverhill to Piermont, running due south-east from Haverhill Corner, a mile and a half from the village, a ledge of mica schist crosses the road, whose strike is N. 25° E., and the dip 45° N. N. W. Three miles out, a second ledge of the same rock crosses, having the same strike and dip, but here becomes more quartzose. This ledge shows striæ running 10° west of north. Three and three quarters miles out, a third ledge crosses, of the same rock, in which are quarries of flagstones and whetstones, the latter known as "Pike's quarry." The excavation here on the south side of the road shows the rock striking due north, and dipping 45° W.

Four and a half miles from Haverhill, in the north-eastern part of Piermont, Eastman's brook passes through the depression between Iron Ore mountain and the northern extension of Piermont mountain. At the falls in this passage is a saw-mill. That part of the ridge north of the stream, in which alone mining has been done, is likewise known by the name of Cross's hill. The first of the old workings, made thirty years ago, is in the open pasture, a few rods below the saw-mill and about thirty feet above the road, from which it is visible. A small outcrop of the ledge has been entered here to the depth of a couple of feet. About 70 feet above this in the edge of the woods is a second working, the most extensive, apparently, which was made. Here the ledge dips 25° S. S. W., with an outcrop of 12 feet perpendicular, in which the working was made laterally some 8 or 10 feet. The mountain, following the same general strike as this ledge, is on its north-west side seamed with numerous parallel outcrops, most of which lie above the one which has been worked. The summit is 250 feet above working No. 2; and from this point the ledge can be seen seaming Piermont mountain in the same manner on the south side of the stream, a quarter of a mile distant. Following the ridge north-easterly, about 50 rods from the end summit and some little distance below the ridge line, in the woods, is working No. 3. Half a mile north-east of the summit, in the edge of the open pasture, near the northern end of a small pond, is working No. 4. Here a cut has been made into the ledge transversely from a point five or six feet below the outcrop on the hillside. All these workings have been upon the same ledge, which runs persistently the whole distance, and indefinitely further with the extension of the mountain.

The rock of the mountain is quartzite, whose numerous outcrops have all the same general strike and dip given above. It is in layers, varying from half a dozen inches to as many feet in thickness, and is generally gray, though in some layers brown in color. At working No. 2, a few feet west of the layer principally worked, is a band one foot wide of pure white quartz, which would serve as an excellent guide in tracing this ore-bearing ledge. Very many of the layers have disseminated through them, in intimate commixture with the quartz, the peroxide of iron in its micaceous form. In the most highly impregnated layers the amount is sufficient to give the cleavage face of the rock the specular lustre and a black color; but its transverse face is a dull gray, from the superabundance of quartz. Most of the ore seems to have been taken out from a layer three feet wide; but this is not specially richer than its neighbors, and its impregnation varies in different places. Nowhere is there a true metallic vein.

The ore, while mingled with quartz beyond the possibility of washing, has none of those impurities which deteriorate the metal. The richest portions might yield as much as 60 per cent. of iron; but the vast mass of the rock would not average 30 per cent. Of the ore, such as it is, there is any amount, for the iron-bearing ledge could doubtless be entered anywhere in its course with substantially the same results as where it has been worked. The ore could not, under the most favorable circumstances, bear transportation.

At Winchester a magnetic ore, carrying 24.26 per cent. of metallic iron, occurs in three beds situated upon the opposite sides of a gneissic anticlinal, whence it is probable that six beds outcrop. The thickest is somewhat less than 40 feet, dipping 40° E., exposed for 200 feet. The smaller beds are five or six feet thick, opened about eight feet deep for 200 feet, and dipping 30°–50° W. These beds were wrought and abandoned before 1800, the ore having been smelted at Furnace village in Winchester.

Of other localities, Thorn mountain in Jackson shows several veins of magnetic ore in granite, from a few inches to two and a half feet wide, running N. 25° W. on the top, and N. 55° W. on the west side of the mountain. Dykes of basalt cut the veins, which afford 37.99 per cent. of metallic iron. The magnetic iron of Unity contains 62.6 per cent. of metallic iron; and the hematite of Lebanon 65.17 per cent. The hematite of Black hill, Benton, yielding 62.4 per cent. of metallic iron, is from six inches to three feet in width, and quite irregular, contained in a granular quartz. Bog ores of considerable amount, containing from 36 to 55 per cent. of metallic iron, are mentioned in the towns of Eaton, Barnstead, Charlestown, Haverhill, Lebanon, Milford, Lancaster, and Pelham. Additional localities of like account, of all three kinds, are in the towns of Warren, Haverhill, Bath, Landaff, Franconia (east part), Lyman, Dalton, Gorham, Berlin, Gilmanton, Moultonborough, Jackson, Pittsfield, Barnstead, Merrimack, Bedford, Amherst, Lyndeborough, Peterborough, Swanzey, Gilford, Freedom, Grafton, Eaton, Enfield, Canaan, and Orford.

The following table gives the results of Dr. Jackson's analyses of iron ores from various parts of the state, some of them said to be of considerable importance:

	Peroxide of iron.	Silica.	Titanic acid.	Vegetable matter.	Manganese.	Sulphuric acid.	Loss, and water.	Metallic iron.
Thorn mountain, Jackson	54.8	43.6	.....	.....	.....	.....	1.6	37.99
Unity—magnetic	90.4	4	6.8	.....	.....	.....	.....	62.6
Winchester—magnetic	34	66.6	.....	.....	.....	.....	.....	24.26
Lebanon—hematite	94	6	.....	.....	.....	.....	.....	65.17
Benton—hematite	90	8	.....	.....	.....	.....	2	62.4
Eaton—bog ore	72	12	.....	12	.....	.....	4	49.92
Barnstead—bog ore	71.6	9.4	.....	9.8	.....	.....	9.2	49.71
Barnstead—nodular	52.8	2.8	.....	10.8	2.4	.....	30	36.5
Charlestown—bog ore	69.4	4.6	.....	18.6	Trace	.48	6.92	48.12
Haverhill—bog ore	72.6	4.6	.....	12.8	.....	.....	10	50.31
Lebanon—bog ore	70.6	7.6	.....	15	.....	.....	5.8	48.65
Milford—bog ore	80	8	.....	8.8	.....	.....	3.2	55.67
Lancaster—bog ore	71.2	2.6	.....	12	.....	.....	14.2	46.56

LEAD.

Lead is very widely disseminated. In nearly every town of the state you will find a tradition to this effect: "A few years since, my uncle, 88 years old, died. He knew of a valuable vein of lead upon the mountain. Was told of it by an Indian, who used to take an axe, chop off a lump of the ore, melt it, and run it into bullets. Uncle never told me exactly where it was, but there must be a magnificent vein of lead on the mountain." Without doubt this is a correct statement, as lead is very common; and those who have patience to explore the mountain over may be rewarded for their pains. With the little space left, I can only briefly mention the most important of our known lead openings. I will commence with a description of the Madison mine, written by me in 1870. Jackson has described this more fully in his report.

Madison Lead Mine. The rock is a quartzite, near an immense sandy plain, where rock exposures are almost unknown. An egg-shaped excavation has been made into this rock not less than forty feet wide, and perhaps sixty feet long by seventy-five deep. The wall rocks have a high westerly dip, and the vein is six feet wide. The ores are galenite and blende, of which only the former is utilized at present. There is a force of twenty-five men employed to mine, raise, sort, and crush the ore, which is sent to New York to be smelted and to be resolved into lead and silver. Prof. Seely's assay of the galenite shows that it contains of silver to the ton of 2000 lbs., ninety-four ounces, eleven pennyweights, and five grains, or nearly eight pounds.

This mine was first worked in 1826. It has been occasionally worked, but never so energetically as at present (1870). There is machinery on the ground worth $50,000, including one steam-engine of eighty horse-power, a second of fifteen, a twenty-four stamp mill and Cornish crushing rolls, capable of crushing a ton of rock in ten minutes. During the past winter the amount of ore dressed to seventy per cent. of lead has averaged one barrel per day. In the spring, and at present, this rate of production has been doubled. The actual selling price is $113 per ton, or $55 for the silver and $58 for the lead.

This mine has also supplied zinc-blende in abundance. No use could be made of it, as, until recently, there were no furnaces in the country capable of reducing it. Not long since 100 barrels of this zinc ore were sold to parties in New Jersey for $6 each, whereas they should have brought as much as $20. Those who have zinc-blende in abundance would do well to save it, and watch the market prices given for it.

A mile east of Madison station, on the Portsmouth, Great Falls & Conway Railroad, not far from the north-east corner of Silver lake, galena has been exploited at several points upon the same mineral belt. This has been proved for as much as three eighths of a mile, within which distance three openings have been made upon it by as many different parties. At the northernmost, known as the "Burke property," the most work has been done, two shafts having been sunk to the depths of 30 and 90 feet respectively. The next opening, going southward, is known as the "Banks shaft," and is 45 feet deep. The next, called the "Hoyt shaft," is down 27 feet. The ground occupied by these three companies is no more than should have been consolidated into one mining property. The vein, so called, is a mineralized band in the ferruginous gneiss of the country, evidently persistent in its occurrence, and believed by some to be the extension of that at the well-known Madison lead mine, which lies four miles to the south-west. The vein strikes N. 15° E., and, like most bedded veins, has a variable dip, ranging in this from 45° to 90° W., at most points nearer the latter. Its substance is quartz, white and gray, spotted frequently with a soft greenish-yellow magnesian mineral. The ores are galenite, blende, and pyrites, preponderating apparently in the order given. In such of the rock thrown out as was visible, they do not occur any of them in large nodules, but scattered in specks through the gangue, and in such form that much would be unavoidably lost in the necessary process of mechanical concentration. A fair average sample, taken from the accessible output of the "Banks shaft," of such rock as would have to be worked, crushed without any separation of ore from gangue, showed,—in the hands of a professional assayer,—gold, 0.01 oz., silver, 3 oz., to the ton of 2000 lbs.

Shelburne Lead Mine. About 1½ miles west of Shelburne station, on the Grand Trunk Railway, Lead Mine brook empties into the Androscoggin on the north side. Following up this brook 1½ miles, a branch comes in from the west through a narrow gorge on the eastern declivity of Mt. Hayes. At the junction of the two brooks are the ruins of ore-separating works, run by water-power, and of three log-cabins. We are here at an elevation of 130 feet above the Androscoggin. Taking the western branch, a further walk of about forty rods brings us to an abrupt turn in the brook at a right angle, the stream coming down over the cliff, which forms the northern wall of the gorge, in a cascade thirty feet high. The mineral vein runs along the bottom of the gorge, much of its course in the very bed of the stream. At the abrupt turn above mentioned the first opportunity to attack it above water-level has been availed of to drive an adit westerly into the mountain upon the vein itself. The adit is 5 feet by 4, and extends about 30 feet. Within a distance of fifteen rods from the adit three shafts have been sunk in the bottom of the narrow gorge, so close to the brook, and their mouths so little above its level, that the most ordinary rise would flood the entire workings. This metalliferous deposit has been worked at several different periods by different companies, and the adit was an after-thought of a later company. One of the shafts is stated to be 80 feet in depth, and another 275, and to have proved the vein eight feet wide at the lowest point reached, carrying in places six inches solid ore. If this be so, the vein at the surface is evidently "a pinch," and the adit could have given no practical vantage without the sinking in it of a winze. At the present not only are the shafts flooded,—they were this probably twenty-four hours after the pumps stopped,—but the floor of the adit is under water, so that it is impossible to learn much of the deposit without a considerable amount of actual work being done. The vein, which is one of segregation, has a strike N. 75° E., and a dip 70° N. 15° W. At its surface its width ranges from two to six inches. The gangue is quartz, which on the hanging-wall is quite pure, while on the foot wall, which is ill defined, it grades into a micaceous gneiss. The chief ore carried is galenite, associated with a very dark blende, and a notable amount of pyrites. The galenite seems to be invariably mixed with these ores, while on the other hand the pyrites occurs in some places unassociated. A sample of galenite with pyrites, gave, in the hands of a professional assayer,—gold, none; silver, 15.06 oz. to the ton of 2000 lbs. This ore was almost free from gangue, and may be considered a favorable sample. From the fact that so many parties have worked this,—one of the historical mines of New Hampshire,—always with the result of abandonment, it would seem a fair inference that however wide the vein may have become in depth, and however rich the ore, the ratio of ore to gangue must have been too small.

Galena has also been exploited during recent years at a point a few miles farther west on Mt. Hayes. The results were unsatisfactory, and the workings unextensive, compared with those just described.

Silverdale Mine. In the south part of Pittsfield, on the Suncook river and the Suncook Valley Railroad, is the hamlet known upon the maps as "Webster's Mills," called more recently upon the neighboring guide-boards, "Silverdale." The exploitation for silver-lead has been on the east side of the river, about one fourth of a mile north of the bridge, upon the first bench above the immediate river-bottom. The southernmost shaft is that at which the most work has been done, and from which the specimens in the state cabinet were taken. A few feet north of this is an untimbered cut, ten feet deep, which simply serves, being dry, to show the vein for that slight depth. Several rods further north is a third opening, known as the "Couch shaft," apparently off the vein. The two shafts are full of water; but a resident of Silverdale, familiar with the workings, states that the first is about 35 and the second about 30 feet deep. The vein is a "bedded" one, and, along with the synchronous country rock, has a general strike N. 34° E., and a dip 85° N. 56° W. It averages two feet wide, the gangue of quartz carrying the ore in perpendicular seams running parallel to the vein walls. The foot-wall on the east is of white gneiss, reticulated with little quartz veins, and its plane of demarcation from the vein is very definitely marked. The hanging-wall is indistinctly defined, the vein-rock grading into a quartz characterized by greenish-yellow and brown patches of softer mineral, sometimes nodular, and sometimes angular in outline. Blende runs through the vein in sheets one half inch thick persistently, occasionally widening into bulges one half foot thick, blotched with large-crystalled galenite. On the border of the vein the rock carries considerable pyrites in minute sprinkled crystals, and occasionally chalcopyrite in small blotches.

A furnace has been erected at the bridge for smelting the galenite under a new patent, said to contain original and valuable features. The furnace-house being locked and the key temporarily out of town the day the locality was examined, no description of it can be given. An assay of the Silverdale ore gave 1.6 ounces of silver to the ton.

Loudon. In the central part of the township of Loudon galena has been exploited at the locality called "Buswell's Mine." The opening is on elevated land, the aneroid showing a height of 300 feet above Pittsfield station on the Suncook Valley Railroad. The shaft was not only full of water, but planked over at the time the spot was visited, so that little idea could be formed of the mine. There is plainly no vein, the opening having been made in what is apparently the rock of the country, though it might, on more extended examination, prove to be an exceedingly wide trappean dyke. This rock has a general strike N. 40° E. and dip 80° N. W. It is porphyritic, the included crystals, most commonly one half inch long and one sixteenth wide, showing very distinctly on surfaces slightly weathered. There is likewise considerable included quartz. The galenite occurs in small blotches, showing a tendency to form in the centre of quartz nodules. It is unusually dark-colored and splendent, plentifully sprinkled with minute crystals of pyrites. The entire quantity of ore is slight.

Rumney. Upon porphyritic gneiss in the north-east part of the town is a vein owned by George L. Merrill. The metalliferous mass is 12 feet wide, exposed in an excavation 14 feet deep. The walls dip 80° N. 70° W., enclosing a soft feldspathic rock with some quartz. Two kinds of trap rocks are situated in the vein, dark- and light-colored. The galena and blende follow reticulating veins of quartz, inter-penetrating the general mass. The galena contains a trace of gold, and 1.95 oz. of silver to the ton.

North Woodstock. Handsome specimens of galena, blende, and pyrites have been shown us from Horner's farm. Some work has been done in the way of opening the vein. The galena shows a trace of gold, and 7.84 oz. of silver to the ton.

Hooksett. Upon the quartz ridge south-west from the Pinnacle is a small lead vein. The best part of it shows three inches width of galena. This is hardly sufficient for mining.

Other localities are in Bath, Haverhill, Epsom, Nashua, Lyndeborough, Dunbarton, Tamworth, Sandwich, Lyme, and elsewhere.

TIN.

Tin ore has been discovered in Jackson in such quantity and so related that miners have thought a good vein of it might be developed by diligent exploitation. From time to time prospectors have searched the neighborhood, particularly in Maine, where greater success has been met with than in our state. Dr. Jackson was greatly interested in the subject, particularly as this was the first discovery of the ore in so great quantity in the country. From investigations made about 1840, the following conclusions have been derived:

The rock of the country is a mica schist dipping 30° N. E. by E., with veins or elvans of granite crossing it. The ore is cassiterite, occurring in four veins, making a triangular space of 200 to 300 square feet by their intersection. No. 1 is mostly compact ore, eight inches in the widest part, yielding 30 per cent. of tin, associated with chalcopyrite and mispickel, and the course is N. 7° E. No. 2 contains crystalline ore with mispickel, half an inch wide, running N. 80° E. in granite. This ore crosses the others, like the horizontal line in a figure 4. No. 3 is a compact ore in mica schist, from half to three quarters of an inch wide, running N. 56° E. No. 4 is nearly parallel to the last, from a half to an inch and a quarter wide. No. 1 is cut by a dyke of trap. The rock near the veins contains from two to ten per cent. of tin. The other minerals found with the cassiterite are mispickel, pharmacosiderite, chalcopyrite, native copper, wolfram, fluor, and molybdenite. In 1843, eleven and a half ounces of ingot tin were obtained from the Jackson ore; but the mine never seems to have been worked steadily, though it was being mined at the time of my visit in 1864.

The following notes in regard to the working of the tin mine were furnished by Mr. George N. Merrill, as also a view of the tin locality, and a profile (Fig. 8) showing the situation of the schist and shafts.

"The American Tin Company was chartered by the legislature of New Hampshire July 15, 1864, and they issued sixty thousand shares at $5 per share. The company actually expended and paid out $4,371.69. The last work done at the mine was in August, 1865. The company sunk two shafts, one twenty-five the other forty-five feet, and made an adit ninety feet. To have reached the main shaft would have required an adit 400 feet in length." The rock excavated from the adit is composed mainly of a uralitic sienite not found elsewhere. This may furnish a clue to the kind of rocks carrying tin.

Fig. 8.—Section of Workings at Tin Mine, Jackson.
Adit, 90 feet. Distance from entrance of adit to main shaft, 400 feet.

Considerable time has been devoted to exploring the country between Madison and Milan, where it was supposed, from the character of the rocks, that tin might be found. In many places there are indications of metallic deposits, but for the most part they are iron sulphides, at least on the surface, while a few blasts might reveal something more valuable. Every new mine that is discovered has characteristics peculiar to itself, and these have to be carefully studied before any one can form a correct judgment in regard to it. Minerals present themselves, too, under so many different phases, and when exposed to the atmosphere are often so changed as scarcely to be recognized, that no one, unless he has made explorations, can form any estimate as to the time required or the labor necessary to be performed. Hence, explorations for tin in New Hampshire require the expenditure of considerable means in costeaning and sinking shafts before it will be possible to pronounce definitely that the metal cannot be found. In going from

Robertson's Corner to Madison Corner, just after passing the height of land south of the road, we find the schist in many places pyritiferous, and often much decomposed. There are also numerous beds of granite, or possibly they may be nothing more than immense veins. The schist, where it does not contain pyrites, is similar to that in Jackson where tin has been found, and here it belongs to the Montalban series. In Jackson, every locality where it was thought there could be any show for tin was examined, and an analysis of many of the specimens collected has been made by Prof. Seely, and very rarely has there been found even a trace of tin. The most promising localities away from the old opening are in the valley immediately north of Thorn mountain and on the west slope of the Black mountain, and the tin rocks here underlie the andalusite schists, at least on south end of Black mountain, and apparently uncomformably. On the west side of Tin mountain, near the Dundee road, the schist is pyritiferous, and there are numerous beds of granite; the rocks seem to be quite similar to those on the opposite side where tin has been found. Going north, the entire western slope of Black mountain, from its base half way up, seems to be composed of pyritiferous schists, beds of granite, and gneiss. There is a promising locality near Mr. J. R. Harriman's; also, near the place formerly occupied by Mr. J. Y. Perkins.

Bismuth, Manganese, Arsenic, and Molybdenum.

Native bismuth has been found upon Sunapee mountain, near Newbury. Nothing further than the fact of its existence is known. Manganese is not common in large amount. Bog manganese is reported in Gilmanton, Grafton, Lisbon, Haverhill, Laconia, Rindge, and Nelson.

In Winchester and Hinsdale is a bed of impure rhodonite 8 feet thick, according to Jackson, enclosed in gneiss, dipping 70° S. 60° E. in the first, and 84° easterly in the second locality. When this mineral is pure, it is highly prized for ornamental purposes.

The arsenical pyrites—mispickel or arsenopyrite—is very common in our state. It is most abundant along the Connecticut valley, both massive and crystallized. Localities of note are Jackson, Francestown, Haverhill, Lebanon, Weare, Groton, Lisbon, Lyman, Middleton, Dunbarton, Epsom, and Alton. Should the manufacture of arsenic ever be called for, New Hampshire can afford a plentiful supply. This mineral is worth studying as a possible source for gold, silver, cobalt, and nickel.

Molybdenum occurs quite abundantly at Westmoreland. Dr. Jackson examined the locality with care, and thinks the mineral is plentiful. It is the sulphuret, associated with blue compact feldspar and quartz containing apatite. Experiments have not been made to satisfy us whether the compounds of this metal can be used successfully as a mordant in the dyeing of cloths. The blue color of the compounds is one of great beauty. The papers have occasionally stated that parties have proposed to reopen the mine and extract the ore, but our visits have never found evidences of recent work there. I annex a careful description of the locality by a friend who visited the place at my request:

The old workings on Lincoln's hill, Westmoreland, in a gneissic rock, which is characterized by a predominance of mica and quartz, the latter having in many spots a bright red color, so that the outcrop is suggestive of ferruginous quartzite. The general course of the ledge is N. 40° E., with a dip of 50° N. W. The outcrop in which the surface work was done is on the side of a slight depression in the hill; and here the rock has been blasted to a depth, on the upper side, of 5 or 6 feet. From this point the ledge can be traced down the hill 270 paces to where it is intersected by a dry water-course, the outlet of the above mentioned depression, beyond which, on the opposite swell, it is not seen. Above the pit outcrops are visible to a yet greater distance on the rising hill. About 50 paces below the pit an adit has been carried into the knoll from the bed of the water-course, which here is parallel with it. The adit bends a little to the east in its further part, but its general course is straight, and may be set down as E. 20° S. It is 4 feet wide, about 6 feet high, and 35 feet long. The precise height it is impossible to give, for the reason that, at the time of its being visited, it was filled with water and ooze to the depth of three feet, with an unknown amount of débris beneath this. The rock is schistose, and notably micaceous at the surface, but at the distance of a dozen feet becomes massive. The walls of the adit are so covered now with the exudations and incrustations of more than thirty years, the period which has elapsed since the abandonment of the work, that it is impossible to tell, without putting in a blast, into what it has been pushed. It is pretty plain, however, from the absence of any seaming of the walls at its further extremity, that it has not entered any vein. In the pit before mentioned the vein exposed is of quartz, about two inches wide, and carries molybdenite, granular and in small scales, often in radiating clusters. In its present appearance, and the character of the loose fragments of the gangue lying in the pit, the vein gives no evidence of richness; but it would be unwarrantable, without clearing and blasting, to express any opinion upon this point.

CHAPTER II.

BUILDING MATERIALS, ETC.

IN this chapter I propose to enumerate the principal quarries whence stones used for building purposes are obtained; mention whatever facts have been obtained respecting the quantity of material sent to market; the names of the companies; number of men employed, etc. The articles used for building are properly granite, slate, flags, clays for brick, limestone, and soapstone. Other useful articles, obtained from the earth for direct use, or capable of special manufacture, are quartz and feldspar for glass; mica, plumbago, precious stones, whetstones, copperas, alum, titanium, polishing powder, moulding sand; and ochre for paint. These all occur abundantly within our limits.

Granite.

So common is this rock that New Hampshire is usually known as the *Granite State.* In every-day life this term is applied to rocks which are not properly granite in the technical sense, as sienite and gneiss, but all of them useful for building. In the stratigraphical and mineralogical parts of our report, different classifications are employed. In the first instance are the Concord, Conway, Albany, Chocorua, and other geographical terms, used for convenience. In the second instance, the names of the peculiar constituent minerals are employed to distinguish them,—as the biotite, muscovite biotite, and hornblende granites. It will be unnecessary in this connection to make extensive use of either of these classifications, though they will be referred to many times.

In every part of the state the common gneiss rocks are used for stone walls and the underpinning of buildings. No mention can be made of such material, but only of those that are of superior quality, or what, on account of convenient situation, have been extensively employed in the villages. I will first mention all the facts in my possession respecting the quarries, their locations, proprietorship, capabilities, etc., reserving any generalizations to subsequent pages. The economic facts have been chiefly collected in the spring of 1878.

A very large number of our quarriers operate upon a stone like that obtained in Concord, and hence familiarly known as the Concord granite, or the muscovite-biotite variety. Those of this character are known in Concord, Hooksett, Salem, Pelham, Nashua, Milford, Fitzwilliam, Troy, Marlborough, Roxbury, Swanzey, Plymouth, Manchester, Farmington, Sunapee, and Mason.

Concord. The granite quarries of Concord are situated one to two miles north-west from the city, on the easterly slopes of Rattlesnake hill. The Concord & Claremont Railroad runs at the north-east foot of this hill, and the granite is loaded upon its cars at points one fourth mile to one mile south-east from West Concord station. Two of the quarries nearest to this station are beside the railroad; the distance teamed from others varies from one eighth to three fourths of a mile.

The largest of these quarries are those of the Concord Granite Company and the Granite Railway Company. Nine other quarries are worked at the present time. The number was somewhat greater in 1873, which was the last of several years marked by unusual business prosperity; and the number of men employed and the value of granite sold by the larger proprietors, all of whom still continue operations, were during these years two or three to ten times as great as now.

Brief notes respecting the Concord quarries are as follows:

Concord Granite Company: Alfred Sampson, president; E. C. Sargent, treasurer and agent. This quarry was first opened about twenty-five years ago; owned as now, with a large business, since 1860. In 1873, about 25 men were employed in quarrying, and 200 in cutting, the annual sales amounting to about $200,000; in 1877 this company have employed about 8 quarrymen and 30 cutters, with sales of $20,000. Largest block quarried, 20 tons; it is claimed that a solid block 100 by 25 by 10 feet could be got at this quarry. Buildings from it are that of the Presbyterian Board ot Education, in Philadelphia; Booth's theatre, in New York; the Advertiser and Herald buildings, in Boston; and the Custom House in Portland.

Granite Railway Company: Henry E. Sheldon, agent. Quarry opened in 1861. In

1873, about 20 quarrymen and 80 cutters were employed, with sales amounting to $200,000; there are now 4 quarrymen and 25 cutters, with a yearly product of $20,000. Largest block, 18 tons; could supply one 40 by 20 by 6 feet in dimension. Buildings from this quarry are the Equitable Life Insurance Co. (above the basement), Staats Zeitung building, and Germania Savings Bank, in New York; the Charter Oak Life Insurance Co. (above the basement), in Hartford; and the City hall and Horticultural hall, in Boston.

Norton & Holmes (formerly, till 1878, P. E. Blanchard's quarry): opened in 1865. In 1873, 20 men were employed in quarrying and 60 in cutting, the yearly sales being about $45,000; they are now $8,000. This quarry supplied the basement and trimmings for the first three stories of the Tribune building, New York; the Washington and Eddy street fronts of the City hall in Providence; Bemis block, near the Transcript building, in Boston; and the Soldiers' monument in Georgetown, Mass.

Donagan & Davis: quarry opened in 1872. In 1873, 15 quarrymen and 4 cutters were employed; sales, $75,000. No quarrying has been done for two years. Some 10 cutters are now employed, the sales being about $10,000. The largest block of granite ever taken from Concord was supplied by this quarry, being the base of the Soldiers' monument at Marlborough, Mass., 8½ feet square by 3½ feet thick, weighing 22¼ tons. Shafts could be got 18 feet long and 4 feet square. The building of the New England Life Insurance Co., in Boston, was from this quarry.

Fuller & Pressy: quarry opened in 1865. In 1873 about 25 men were employed in quarrying, the sales amounting to $20,000; now 15 men are employed, the sales being about $7,000, all unhammered stone. The largest blocks supplied have weighed 15 to 20 tons; shafts could be got 18 feet long and 3 feet square. Jordan & Marsh's building in Boston is from this quarry; also, the Manchester, N. H., Soldiers' monument.

Abijah Hollis: quarry opened in 1865. In 1873, 12 men were employed in quarrying; at present about 8 are at work. All the stone is sold rough. Largest blocks ever sent away, 18¾ tons; could get a block measuring 100 by 30 by 12 feet. Examples of the stone from this quarry are the Ether monument, Boston public garden; the Cadet monument, Mount Auburn cemetery; and the Soldiers' monument at Concord, Mass.

Gay Brothers: quarry opened in 1865; purchased by present owners in 1876. Men employed in 1873 and now, about 6,—all in quarrying.

Crowley & Quinn: quarry opened in 1864. In 1873, 10 men, all at quarrying, with sales amounting to $5,000; in 1877, 3 in quarrying and 4 in cutting, with sales of about $3,000. Largest block, 10½ by 5 by 3½ feet; could supply shaft 20 feet long and 3 feet square.

Putney & Nutting: quarry opened about 1850. In 1873, 6 men were employed, all in quarrying, with $5,000 sales; now, very little is done. The Masonic Temple in Boston is from this quarry.

G. W. Emerton: quarry opened in 1875; 5 quarrymen and 5 cutters; yearly sales, about $8,000.

Charles A. Bond: quarry opened in 1877, employing 5 men.

The principal dealers in hammered granite in Concord, not owning quarries, are P. E. Blanchard, who employs 15 men at stone-cutting; Hunton & Perry, 18 men; John H. Flood, 15 men; Blanchard & McAlpine, 10 men; and Flanders & Gannon, 12 men.

Hooksett. In Hooksett two granite quarries are worked. They are near together on the east side of the Merrimack, two miles south of the village and about half a mile from the Concord Railroad. The upper quarry, which yields the finer stock, was opened as much as fifty years ago. For several years past it has been worked by Oliver Gay, by whom the lower quarry, used principally for bridge masonry and rough work, was opened in 1873. At that time 30 men were employed in quarrying and 10 in cutting. In 1877 both these quarries were purchased by A. L. Waite, who employed last year about 15 men, principally in quarrying. Proprietors in 1878, Bonney & Waite.

Salem. A quarry in Salem, opened about forty years ago, owned since 1870 by David Nevins, of Methuen, is situated one third mile west-south-west from Salem depot. Ten quarrymen were employed here several years ago, but very little is done now.

A visit to the Nevins quarry, in 1875, showed that the rock is strictly gneiss, dipping 50° N. 70° W., with prominent vertical joints running N. 65° W. There was a cap of poor rock overlying the workable stone, requiring removal before good material could be obtained. This was 25 feet thick in some places. Both the horizontal and vertical joints exist here. The opening is shaped like the letter L, 300 feet long, measuring both arms, and 100 feet wide. The ground is low, so that pumping is required to remove the water.

Pelham. In Pelham, the greater part of the quarries are on Gage's hill, two miles east-north-east from the village. The nearest railroad stations are Salem and Messer's, on the Manchester & Lawrence Railroad, four and a half miles distant. A proposed railroad from Nashua to Plaistow would pass at the north foot of this hill. The distance to be teamed from the different quarries would then vary from one eighth of a mile to one mile.

The largest business here is that of Bodwell & Webster, for whom Samuel Kelley is agent. This quarry was opened about 1850. It has been under the present owners since 1873. In 1874 and 1875 about 6 men were employed in quarrying and 4 in cutting, the annual sales being about $8,000. Last year the sales were about $3,000. Largest blocks quarried, about 4 tons; could supply shafts 15 feet long and 3 feet square. The granite is bedded in sheets varying from 6 inches to 3½ feet in thickness. This company owns a tract of 80 acres.

Other quarries on this hill are those of Benjamin D. Kittredge, employing about 5 men; Abner Kittredge, 3 or 4 men; D. H. Webster & Son, 4 men; Gage & Woodbury, 4 men; J. N. Woodman, 5 men; John Roney and Moses Johnson, each 2 men.

This granite finds a market principally in Lawrence, Haverhill, and vicinity. Lawrence dam is built of it; and most of the stone caps and sills used in these cities are supplied from Gage's hill. The stone is of fine quality, well suited for cemetery and building purposes. The earliest quarrying upon this hill was in 1782, by Abel Gage. Two other quarries are situated in Pelham, 1¼ and 1½ miles south-east from the village. The former is owned by Oscar F. Carlton, who employed 5 men in 1873, but does very little work now. The latter is owned by Calvin Coburn, who, in 1873, had about 15 quarrymen and 5 cutters. This quarry supplied the stone for the Lowell water-works. The granite of both quarries goes principally to Lowell, being teamed 5 miles. It is mostly used for rough masonry and edge-stones. The proposed Windham & Lowell Railroad will run near these quarries.

Nashua. A quarry, half a mile south-west from the city, on land of the Nashua Manufacturing Company, and opened by them in 1823, has been leased and operated by C. W. Stevens since 1872. About 6 men are employed in quarrying and 3 in cutting. The sales in 1873 were about $10,000; last year, $6,000. Used mostly for bridge masonry, edge-stones, and foundations. Largest blocks, 6½ feet square by 1½ feet thick; and slabs, for cemetery borders or for underpinning, 20 feet long.

Milford. This town has numerous granite quarries, several having been recently opened. Brief notes of them are as follows:

Luther M. Burns, 2 miles south-south-west from the village: qurrry opened 75 years ago, being the oldest in Milford; owned as now since 1862. In 1873, 12 men were employed, the annual sales amounting to about $15,000. Last year the sales were only $2,000. Largest blocks sold have been 28 feet long, for borders of cemetery lots; shafts, 15 feet long and 2 feet square, could be supplied. The town-house in Wakefield, Mass., is trimmed from this quarry.

Nathan Merrill: quarry near the foregoing, opened in 1873. Workmen, 3; annual sales, about $1,500. Blocks 20 feet long and 2 to 3 feet square can be supplied. The basement and steps of the Baptist church in Milford, N. H., and one of the buildings of the Bigelow Carpet Company, of Clinton, Mass., are from this quarry. The proposed Manchester & Fitchburg Railroad would go near these quarries.

Thomas M. King: quarry half a mile south-east from the village, and about an eighth of a mile from the railroad; opened in 1870; owned as now since 1874. Workmen, 7; yearly sales, about $2,500,—one half being dimension stone, the rest being used for cellar walls and similar work. This granite is finer grained than most of the quarries in this town. Much of it lies in straight sheets, 6 inches to 1 foot thick, from which heavy flagstones, of any size up to 20 feet square, can be obtained. In another part of the quarry the beds are thicker, and can supply monumental shafts 3 or 4 feet square. The fire engine building in Lowell, and Merchants' Exchange in Nashua, are trimmed with this stone.

William Jones: quarry on south side of Souhegan river, 4 miles west of the village; opened in 1875. Yearly sales, about $1,000.

The following are on the north side of Souhegan river:

Everett Hutchinson: quarry 1 mile north-west of the village; opened about 1870; 5 workmen; yearly sales, about $2,000.

Daniel A. Bates: quarry about 2 miles north-west of village; opened in 1866, being the first quarry north of the river; owned as now since 1874; workmen, about 5; sales yearly, $3,000, formerly (in 1874) $8,000.

George F. Parker: quarry near the last; opened in 1869; annual product, formerly, $4,000, now $1,200.

Albert Carlton: near the foregoing; opened in 1876; workmen, 2; annual sales, about $1,500.

Kittredge & Palmer: same locality; opened in 1874; annual sales, about $1,500.

Parker Fletcher: same locality; annual sales, about $1,000.

Newton Perham: quarry in edge of Amherst, teaming to Milford; yearly product, about $1,000.

Granite dealers in Milford, who dress the stone but do not own quarries, are Isaac H. Carlton, Charles S. Barnes, Marvell & Weaver, Pierce Perham, and Frank Frost.

Fitzwilliam. The granite quarries in Fitzwilliam are principally situated beside or near the railroad in the vicinity of the depot. Brief notes respecting them are as follows:

Daniel H. Reed: quarries one half mile south of the depot; opened in 1816; owned and worked as now since 1864, on a tract of 300 acres, mostly of granite suitable for quarrying. Five openings are now worked, two of them supplying large amounts. Quarrymen, 10 to 30; average number of cutters, 5. Sales in 1869, $40,000; now, about $15,000 yearly. A part of this granite lies in straight sheets, varying in thickness from a few inches to a foot, from which flagstones of any desired extent can be obtained. Largest block sold, 12 feet long by 4 feet square, weighing 16 tons; largest sheet, 16 by 9 by 1 foot. The statues on Horticultural hall in Boston, and St. Paul's church in Worcester, are from this granite.

Albert Hayden: quarry one fourth mile north of the depot; opened in 1872; 6 workmen; yearly sales, about $5,000. Kruff's block, Pearl street, Boston, was from this quarry.

A. D. Stone & Company: quarry about 1½ miles north of Fitzwilliam village, teaming to Troy depot, 2 miles. Workmen, formerly, 20; no work done last year.

The following quarries are beside the railroad, one mile west of Fitzwilliam depot:

Ethan Blodgett & Company: quarry opened in 1867. Average number of quarrymen, 16; of cutters, 9. Sales in 1873, about $20,000; last year, $12,000. Largest block, 10 by 7 by 2⅝ feet, weighing 15½ tons. Shafts 20 feet long by 3½ feet square can be supplied. Specialty, monumental and cemetery work. T. K. Earle's house in Worcester, the court house in Fitchburg, and the trimmings of Morse Institute in Natick, Mass., are from this quarry.

R. L. Angier: quarry opened in 1865. Average number of quarrymen, 8; of cutters, 8. Value of product in 1873, $10,000; in 1877, $6,000. Largest block, 16 feet long by 2½ feet square, weighing 15 tons; could supply 20 feet long by 3 feet square; has sold blocks 6 feet square and 2 feet thick; could supply 10 feet square and 3 feet thick. Trimmings of Murdock block, and of the National Bank, in Winchendon, Mass., and the Soldiers' monument in Granville, N. Y., are from this quarry.

The Flint quarry, Thomas Hale, agent: not worked last year. Formerly, 15 workmen; yearly sales amounting to about $12,000.

Mr. J. H. Bigelow, freight clerk at Fitzwilliam depot, states the total amount of granite freighted from this town during the last five years to be as follows: in 1873, 13,083 tons; in 1874, 8,103 tons; in 1875, 5,952 tons; in 1876, 6,867 tons; in 1877, 5,923 tons.

Mr. Reed and Mr. Angier can supply a dark variety of granite, containing a large proportion of black mica. This is chiefly used for trimmings. Polishing is done by Mr. Hayden and by Mr. Angier. All the quarrymen of this town sell their granite rough or dressed, as purchasers wish. J. E. Fisher & Co., at Fitzwilliam depot, are also dealers in hammered granite, employing 5 cutters.

Troy. Two quarries have been worked in Troy. One, owned by D. M. Woodward, of Worcester, Mass., is situated three fourths of a mile east of the village; opened in 1871; formerly 5 men, all in quarrying; no work done last year. The Bank block in Fitchburg, Mass., was from this quarry. The other, owned by Luther Whittemore, is half a mile south-east of the village. Average number of quarrymen, 3; not much done last year.

Marlborough. This town has one granite quarry, 1¼ miles north-east from the depot. It is owned by A. G. Mann, of Worcester, Mass. This quarry was opened as early as 1812; under present owners since 1868. The number of quarrymen has varied from 10 to 40; the cutting is mostly done at Worcester. This granite lies in sheets which vary from 3 inches to 3 or 4 feet in thickness. Largest blocks sold, 12 tons; sheets have been split out 70 feet long and 6 feet wide. A considerable part of the sales here has been of paving-blocks, 7 inches square and 4 inches thick. The Union depot at Worcester (except trimmings, which were from Fitzwilliam), and the Stone mill at Harrisville, came from this quarry.

Roxbury. The south-west corner of Roxbury has valuable granite quarries. The largest is that of the Keene Granite Company, H. A. Bodwell, president, E. S. Bodwell, treasurer. This quarry is 2½ miles north-east from South Keene station, where the company's stone-sheds are located. The proposed Manchester & Keene Railroad will run three fourths of a mile distant. Quarry opened about 1850; owned as now, and business greatly increased, since 1872. This company own 227 acres of land, with a right to quarry on 150 acres more. They employed formerly 150 quarrymen and 200 cutters, their sales in 1873 being about $350,000. Largest blocks sold, 12 tons; a sheet now split out would yield a block 30 by 15 by 6 feet in dimensions. Most of the granite quarried by this company has been used in building the new state house at Albany, N. Y. At present, very little work is done here.

The Cheshire Granite Company, S. G. Griffin, president, has a quarry a third of a mile west of the last; only a small amount of work done.

Another quarry, opened about 1840, now owned by John L. Randall, of Albany, N. Y., is situated one mile north-east from these, being about four miles from Keene. It has been worked since 1873 by Nourse & Dean, of Keene, who several years ago employed 6 quarrymen and about 10 cutters. No quarrying of importance done last year. This granite lies in sheets which vary from 6 inches to 8 feet in thickness. Largest blocks moved from the quarry, 12½ feet long by 2½ feet square; shafts 30 to 40 feet long and 4 to 6 feet square could be got. The Episcopal and Baptist churches, and the depot in Keene, are trimmed with stone from this quarry.

Swanzey. Nourse & Dean also lease a quarry, opened in 1863, near Westport station in Swanzey. It is one half mile from the railroad. About 6 men were employed here last year. The Episcopal church in Keene is built from this quarry. R. Stewart, superintendent of Cheshire Railroad, sent the following statement about the granite business along his railroad for the year ending April 30, 1871:

* * * "The largest proportion of the Fitzwilliam stone is sent to Boston, Worcester, and Lowell; while considerable from that point, as well as Marlborough, is seeking a market at Springfield, Hartford, New Haven, and other points reached by Connecticut River Railroad. The stone from Troy is sent principally to Fitchburg for building purposes. The tonnage for the year is as follows: Fitzwilliam, 9,458 tons; Troy, 1,717 tons; Marlborough, 3,292 tons; Keene, 1,040 tons; Westport, 652 tons; total, 16,139 tons. There are occasional shipments to local stations that would, I think, on actual figures of everything, show from 18,000 to 20,000 tons sent."

Plymouth. Four miles north-west from Plymouth are valuable granite quarries, first opened by H. W. Blair, in 1870. They are one half mile north of the Boston, Concord & Montreal Railroad, from which a branch track runs to the quarries. Since 1872 they have been owned and worked by Sanborn & Blair, employing from 5 to 20 men, with average yearly sales of about $4,500. The greater part of this granite is used for bridge masonry. It is also employed in cemetery work, and in building. It lies in sheets 2 to 10 feet in thickness, and slabs of fine stock 20 feet long can be supplied.

Manchester. Two quarries are being worked in a bunch of granite upon the company hill,—one, the Amoskeag quarry, and the other, Bodwell's. The latter's excavation was about 25 feet long, 150 wide, and from 10 to 50 feet deep, three years since. The company's quarry was not so large. Both were being worked energetically, as there is a great demand for stone in the largest city of the state. The stone is inferior to the Concord, though resembling it, being coarser, breaks more readily, and shows a slight tendency to crumble. Other quarries are about Rock Rimmon, on the west side of the Merrimack river, and in the very twisted ancient gneiss between Hallsville and Massabesic lake. The foundations of the city hall, and much of the curbstone in the streets, are of this latter material. The Rimmon stone is granite of rather inferior quality, containing bits of pyrites.

Mason. An extensive business is carried on at the Glen quarry in Mason, owned by A. Macdonald, of Mt. Auburn, Mass. It is situated close to the Peterborough & Shirley Railroad, in the east part of the town. There are two principal openings. The one I saw is the more southerly, estimated to be 300 feet long, 150 wide, and 40 deep. The surface shows slightly the breakage by ice in the glacial period, like that observed in Manchester. From 25 to 30 workmen were employed in 1877. Steam is used extensively. To the east is a larger opening, capable of furnishing obelisks 60 feet long. A large monument has been erected of this granite at Greenville, Penn. There are many of various sizes at Mt. Auburn. A very pretty building, belonging to the Delta Psi Society, is being built of this stone at Hartford, Conn. The joints in this quarry are somewhat irregular. Seams of kaolin clay occasionally occur in them. There are other quarries farther north along the railroad, doing less business than the one described.

Sunapee. There is considerable quarrying done at Sunapee Harbor, very near the lake, on Keyser hill. A variety nearly black is found here, which is properly mica schist, not granite, in connection with a variety very like that of Concord. (See Vol. II, p. 510.) It is marked on the county map as the Bailey quarry.

Farmington. There is plenty of excellent granite in Farmington, hardly distinguishable from the Concord stone. The area, as shown by the atlas map, is not large, but it is sufficiently so for all practical purposes. The quarries are about a mile and a half north-west from the depot, and were being successfully worked at the time of my visit in 1875.

Miscellaneous Granites.

Several different kinds of granite are quarried in various parts of the state, the most important of which will be mentioned. One not very different in external appearance from the Concord is that of Haverhill.

Haverhill. In the edge of Piermont, two miles south of Haverhill, are two granite quarries, known as the Catamount and Black Hill quarries, owned by James Barstow and W. H. Page. These quarries have been worked more or less for nearly 100 years. They have been for several years leased to Daniel J. Winn & Co., of Haverhill, who employed 4 men in quarrying and cutting in 1873, with sales amounting to $2,000; last year 7 men were employed, the sales being about $3,000. The Catamount stone is used principally for bridge masonry and similar purposes. The Black Hill stone is adapted for the finer kinds of cemetery and ornamental work. Blocks 30 feet long and 5 feet square could be got from the latter quarry.

Another granite quarry is worked by Hubert Eastman near North Haverhill. It has been worked more or less since 1840, and the sales for some seasons have amounted to $400. The stones have been used principally for buildings and bridge masonry. The largest block split out measured 60 by 4 by 4, tapering to a point. Has been used at Lisbon, Bath, and the adjoining Vermont towns. Has never been used for cemetery monuments.

Columbia Granite. Near Colebrook, just in the edge of Columbia, is a small area of hornblende sienite, wrought as granite by George Parsons, of Colebrook. Its mineral character has been described by Mr. Hawes. The peculiarities are the presence of calcite and liquid carbonic acid. It is easily worked and handsome, coarsely crystalline like the Quincy granite of Massachusetts. It would make an excellent stone for ornamental pillars, especially for inside work. Most of the blocks quarried are used at Colebrook for buildings, not for cemeteries, the stone from Brunswick, Vt., along the Grand Trunk Railway, supplying that want. A few years since Mr. Parsons employed from 6 to 8 hands constantly; now only half that number is needed. Blocks of any size that can be conveniently handled can be quarried here. There have been as yet no orders for this stone from any distant locality requiring railroad transportation. The Brunswick granite is related to that from Concord, and, being favorably situated as regards transportation, is used extensively in northern New England.

St. Johnsbury Granite Company. This concern uses granite from several localities, making a specialty of monumental work. They use most extensively a biotite granite from Blue mountain, Ryegate (one that cuts the Calciferous mica schist); and, on account of the strong contrast between the white feldspar and the black mica, it has a very clean aspect. By leaving the letters and ornamental work raised and polished, an interesting effect is produced, as it makes a strong contrast with the main body of the stone. It receives and retains a high polish. Their gray granite comes from Brunswick, Vt. They are also beginning to use a red biotite granite from Stark, the same with one that has been described in the other parts of this report. It resembles somewhat the red Scotch granite, but is superior to the imported article, because it is finer, and is not permeated with the "pin-holes" constantly occurring in the other. This company is doing a large business. They have a mill for polishing granite close by the St. Johnsbury depot, using steam, and employ a large number of workmen. The use of the "Conway granite" from Stark is the only known instance of the extensive employment of this variety of stone from a New Hampshire locality. There is a good mass of it at Biddeford, Me., that is extensively used.

I have the following additional statements respecting the St. Johnsbury Granite Co., from R. W. Laird, treasurer. The Blue mountain granite requires 2½ miles of transportation to the railroad. It is entirely free from iron, and blocks may be quarried 300 to 400 feet long and ten feet square. Monuments made of the three granites were exhibited at the Centennial exhibition at Philadelphia, and the red Stark stone received a medal and diploma, with the following award: "For the good quality of the material, the originality of design, and the workmanship of the articles exhibited." 80 workmen are employed in April, to be increased in the summer to 100. Monuments are sent to every part of the country, especially the Middle states. The red granite is wrought from boulders.

Lebanon Granite. This may be taken to represent a type of granite very unlike any others that have been mentioned, and it is worked at Walling's quarry in Lebanon; at Freeman's, one less extensively opened, further north in the same town; on Corey hill, and other places in Hanover and Enfield. It is properly a protogene gneiss. It is a heavy, massive stone, better capable of sustaining weight than the Concord variety. S. H. Walling & Son do a large business, and supply the wants of Lebanon, mainly, for building purposes. Stone of very large size can be obtained here. The rock is free from iron pyrites. This cannot be said of the Hanover stone, which was used for the basement of Culver Hall.

One thing should be said of this impurity in the Hanover rock. There is a building on Corey hill containing pieces of the pyrrhotite as large as beechnuts, and though the house has been standing nearly seventy years, there are scarcely any iron stains upon it. This species of pyrites sustains itself so well that oftentimes its presence need not be feared. A more remarkable instance of the ability of this pyrites to resist decomposition may be seen in the Francestown soapstone. I have examined many of the stoves manufactured from this stone, and noticed that bright particles of this pyrites were thickly sprinkled through it. I have also looked at pieces of this steatite that had been subjected to great heat for a long time without much change. It would appear, therefore, that this mineral may not be injurious to granites, as it seems to withstand successfully the vicissitudes of both heat and cold.

Porphyritic Gneiss. This is only employed locally. I have been greatly pleased with the appearance of curbs and foundation stones of this granite, as seen commonly at Lake Village and Meredith. The large rectangular white feldspar crystals render the stone attractive. There is a gray Scotch granite with these reddish-white crystals scattered through it, which is like our porphyritic gneiss. Those who desire a new variety may be pleased with this. The town of New Hampton abounds with handsome ledges of this rock; but any of the areas thus designated upon the map will furnish to a careful search very attractive blocks.

The White Mountain Granites. By these I mean the Conway, Albany, Chocorua, and sienite groups, of which whole mountains stand ready to be quarried, and thus be made serviceable to civilization. Of these, certain portions of the first are unsuitable for building purposes or monuments, because they disintegrate so readily. This has been explained (Part iv, p. 195) by the presence of innumerable pores in the feldspar which admit water charged with carbonic acid, and thus gradually impair the integrity of the stone. But all the Conway granite mountains are not of this character. The other varieties are also capable of furnishing peculiar grades of building stone, and perhaps the time is not far distant when their beauties will be discovered and utilized. Railroads now thread among the mountains, so that new quarries of stone can be easily transported to market. There are fine-grained varieties of the Conway species near the Portland & Ogdensburgh Railroad in the Notch, which are durable. A very handsome stone of this sort has been used by Dr. S. A. Bemis for his dwelling, though more care might have been taken to secure a material free from pyrites.

It was my intention to have presented statements respecting the points to be observed in selecting a good granite for quarrying, the application of microscopic study, and a comparison of our stone with the Scotch, Massachusetts, and other kinds of building material, particularly with reference to strength and ability to resist decomposition. The reader may consult Part IV for a part of this intended sketch, and the rest in general treatises upon building materials, since the size of this volume is already too great.

SLATE.

The only formation likely to furnish quarries of roofing-slate is the Cambrian range along Connecticut river. The Vermont portion has quarries upon it in Guilford and Thetford. There have been several quarries upon this belt in our state, at Littleton, Hanover, and Lebanon, but no work has been done upon any of them for several years. The stone is not quite so good as that in western Vermont or Maine, but certain portions might be utilized in several localities for home purposes, especially for curbs, platforms, tables, flags, etc. In Littleton are two openings in the north part of the town, upon the adjacent farms of Richard Smith and Mr. Bachelder. The band of rock suitable for working is nearly an eighth of a mile wide, and the principal opening has been excavated to the depth of 20 or 25 feet. Bachelder's quarry is the farthest from the road, and has had the most work done upon it. The strata are vertical, and, as the outcrops are on a hill, the facilities for drainage are good, and working surfaces can be obtained 100 feet in depth. The rock seemed to be free from pyrites, was soft, but does not cleave so thin as the slate from Maine. About two miles westerly from Littleton village is a large excavation on the west side of the Blueberry mountain range, high up, and well situated for mining. The opening is about 200 feet long and 50 deep, presenting a face of these dimensions. There is a cross cut into this opening through which the slates are transported over a tramway. Several houses have been erected for the accommodation of the workmen, and a large amount of rock has already been removed. The samples of slate stored for shipment appear to be of excellent quality. The color is a bright dark blue, and the stone soft, and apparently durable. The face corresponds with the front of the hill, so that the position is a favorable one for mining, the slate standing about perpendicular. Thirteen years since, an attempt was made to form a company to work the quarry, but for some reason it failed. Many of the layers are filled with cubical crystals of pyrites, and it is likely that the abundance of this mineral discouraged the proprietors, preventing the carrying on of a large business.

In East Lebanon a company has expended $25,000 upon opening a quarry and erecting a mill, but the work is now abandoned. The property consists of 100 acres of land, about 100 rods in length, along the course of the slate, with a fine water-power,—the Mascomy river,—and situated by the track of the Northern Railroad. Over $4,000 has been spent in opening the quarry, under the superintendence of E. L. Cleaveland, presenting a vertical face about 55 feet broad and deep. I saw slabs 15 feet square, and others, larger, can be obtained. The valuable part of the bed is 30 feet in width. The mill on the Mascomy is 44 feet wide, 65 feet long, and three stories high. It contains machinery driven by water-power, put in at an expense of $8,000, requiring the services of 20 workmen when fully equipped. The slate is not used for roofing, as it does not split sufficiently thin, but may be used for the manufacture of chimney pieces, table-tops, shelves, etc., and marbleized like the slate of western Vermont, where this business has been successfully conducted for many years. The other uses of the stone are for sinks, cisterns, burial cases, flooring, tiling, etc.; and the waste is ground and bolted into slate flour, of which the company sold 150 tons in 1868. In continuing the quarrying, some difficulties arose requiring a further outlay of capital, insomuch that the company became discouraged and suspended operations, the superintendent having accepted a position at the Copperas Hill establishment at Strafford, Vt.

Other openings have been made upon Moose mountain, Hanover, and Croydon mountain in Cornish.

Flags. Such slates and schists as are suitable for flagstones are chiefly what have been described under the Cambrian and Coös schists of the Connecticut valley. They are all comparatively soft, and will not compare for durability with the blue stone from Hudson river, which is used so commonly in the larger towns of lower New England. All stones of this sort that have been quarried in our state are only used locally.

LIMESTONE.

Haverhill. In the east part of Haverhill is a large bed of grayish-white limestone situated in gneiss. It is about a mile and a half from the East Haverhill station, on the Boston, Concord & Montreal Railroad. There are several openings in the bed. The rock is partly bluish-gray, resembling that wrought at Thomaston, Maine, and partly white and coarsely crystalline. It has been seen for 800 feet in length and 400 in width. Dr. Hayes's analysis of it is the following: Carbonate of lime, 94.04; carbonate of magnesia, 1.36; carbonate of iron, .58; phosphate of lime, .22; quartz, silica and mica, 3.80=100. "This sample was variegated gray in color, and contained the quartz, silica and mica as rock mixture. It will afford 53.7 per cent. of lime, to which will be added four parts only of earthy matter. Much of the lime in the market contains 27 per cent. of earthy and foreign matter. Some samples I saw of the limestone contained less earthy matter than the sample analyzed."

In 1864 a pamphlet was prepared by Nicholas Mason, descriptive of the properties and capabilities of this stone, from which it appears that the entire cost of making the lime was 30 cents per cask. At Rockland, Maine, the corresponding expense is given by Alden Ulmer, inspector, at 80 cents per cask.

Lisbon Limestone. In Lisbon lime is also manufactured by Orren Bronson to the amount of 2,200 casks annually. The bed is shown on the several maps to extend several miles through the eastern part of the town, and to crop out on different stratigraphical lines. The thickness is not so great as in Haverhill, but great enough to supply a kiln for many years. Some parts of it were thought to approach 100 feet in thickness. Four different quarries were wrought forty years since, consisting of Mr. Bronson's, Thomas Priest's, David Priest's, and Uriah Oakes's,—the others to the north-east of the first, and within four miles' distance. The T. Priest bed is 13 feet wide; it has been explored for 300 feet in length, and can be wrought to the depth of 60 feet without the necessity of pumping. There is a slight curvature to the bed. As shown on the map, the range continues to the furnace in Franconia, broken twice. The opening north of Sugar hill supplied the furnace with material for fluxing the iron ore. There is another range of limestone parallel with the Bronson-Oakes belt, about two miles to the north-west, following a back road from Salmon Hole brook to the South Branch. Quartzite is associated with it.

Orford and Lyme. In Orford and Lyme is another development of limestone identical in character and geological position with those of Haverhill and Lisbon, and it is essentially continuous for 10 miles near the west edge of the gneiss. On the west side of Cuba mountain a bed has been wrought at intervals for fifty years. Some of the beds are 20 feet thick, and several run close together, as at Tillotson's quarry, where the aggregate thickness of the limestone is 38 feet. I suppose there must be beds of limestone upon Lime hill, though none are marked there upon the map. On the Charles Scott place, in Lyme, are beds 6 feet in thickness. Massive garnet and crystals of hornblende occur in connection with the enclosing beds. Dr. Jackson describes a mixture of limestone and granular quartz on the same farm 120 feet in thickness. Analysis shows it to be quartz mixed with silicate and carbonate of lime. It consists of silica, 80.40; lime, 14.72; magnesia, 1.12; oxide of iron, 0.88; carbonic acid, 2.88=100. It was recommended for the manufacture of glass. On Holt's hill is a bed of limestone one foot thick, in company with iron pyrites. The limestone crops out conspicuously in East Lyme where the road branches to Dorchester and Canaan. The region of these limestone beds in Orford and Lyme is now very sparsely inhabited, insomuch that the road at the west base of Smart mountain is almost impassable.

Littleton. Lime has been burnt in the Helderberg limestones of Littleton in at least two places. One is about three miles to the north of the village on Burnham's hill. Two extensive openings occur here, showing a breadth of stone from 10 to 60 feet thick. The other locality is on Parker brook, about a mile west from the depot. Both these kilns were in action some thirty years since, and produced an excellent quality of lime. It was brown after burning, but slacked white. The amount of the stone is abundant, as has been mentioned in the discussion of the Helderberg formation. The stone near Parker river is unusually white. Another mass of stone, seemingly 40 feet wide and of better quality than the last, occurs on Fitch hill, a mile south-west from the brook locality. This rock forms a knob in a pasture beyond the best fossil outcrop. Still another opening occurs back of J. K. Corey's house, in the south part of the town, near the Ammonoosuc river. By examining the geological map, one will see that the Helderberg group extends southerly upon both flanks of Blueberry hill; and good outcrops of limestone may be looked for in almost any part of the blue-colored areas. That for a mile along the river in North Lisbon is largely composed of a white limestone, but it is not free from silica and rock, and would not answer so well for the manufacture of quicklime.

It is our belief that nearly all the beds mentioned are capable of furnishing a good quality of lime. It is equally strong with that furnished from Maine, but usually makes a brown mortar like that from Weathersfield, Vt., which, by the way, is exactly the same material as the Haverhill and Lisbon stones. Because the mortar is not a pure white it has fallen into disuse, and the Maine or Vermont limes employed instead for finishing. Our stone would furnish good material for three fourths of the plastering needed for houses, or it may be used for agricultural purposes. As it is inexhaustible, there is no reason why the farmers should not order it in large quantities.

At Lime pond, in Columbia, the marl has been used to some extent for the manufacture of quick lime. This article is fully equal to the best imported variety; but the supply is not inexhaustible.

Limestone occurs in many other towns in New Hampshire, but in a comparatively impure condition. It occurs in Plainfield, Cornish, Claremont, Clarkesville, Stewartstown, Amherst, Warner, Wakefield. I append a few analyses of some of these rocks, by Dr. Jackson:

	Silica, mica, etc.	Carbonate of lime.	Carbonate of magnesia.	Iron oxide and alumina.	Carb. iron and manganese.	Carbon.	Magnesia.	Percentage of lime.	
Haverhill—first quality	.5	99.3	......	......	0.2	....	....	55.7	=100
Haverhill—second quality	3.80	90.66	......	......	5.54	....	....	51.03	=100
Thomas Priest, Lisbon	8.2	90.18	......	......	1	....	....		=100
David Priest, Lisbon	15.6	81.6	......	......	2.8	....	....	45.6	
Uriah Oakes, Lisbon—flux	20	80	......	......	2	....	....	43.9	=100
Lyme	25.7	71.7	......	......	2.60	....	....	40.35	=100
Lyme—dark colored	15	83.6	......	......	1.2	2	....	47.04	=100
Orford	64	90	......	4	......	....	....	50.66	=110.4
Amherst	21	75.2	......	2.4	......	..	....	42.32	=98.6
Warner—white crystalline	33	56.4	......	......	......	....	10.8	31.74	=100.2
Warner—gray siliceous	72	10	13	3.2	......	....	....	5.62	=98.2
Cornish—Judge Jackson	31	58.6	1.6	7.8	......	....	....	32.98	=99.2
Lunenburg, Vt	40.6	47.6		11	......	....	....		=99.2
Plainfield	25	23.8	46.6	2.8	......	....	....	13.39	=98.3
Cornish—Johnson's quarry	59.6	22.6	13.8	3.8	......	....	....	15.72	=99.8

Brick Clay.

A few facts have been acquired relative to the manufacture of bricks in the state. They relate to the largest establishments.

The extensive deposit of clay in Pembroke, Allenstown, and Hooksett, has been described on page 94 of Part III. The brick-makers find a slight difference between the gray and blue clays,—the latter requiring more sand to be mixed with it, and shrinking more in burning. Brief notes respecting the manufacture of brick in these towns are as follows:

Natt & William F. Head, Hooksett, make about five millions of brick yearly, employing 60 men. Their market value, loaded on cars, has ranged from $6 to $10 per thousand. They are sold largely in Manchester, Nashua, Lowell, Lawrence, and Worcester.

Jesse Gault, Hooksett, manufactures three to four millions yearly, employing 40 men.

Other brick-yards are those of William G. Andrews, Hooksett, employing 5 men; Jabez Green, Suncook, 5 men; Charles Bailey, Suncook, 5 men; Philip & Warren Sargent, Suncook, 20 men; Edmund Elliott, Pembroke, 5 men; Henry T. Simpson, Pembroke, 20 men. These yards will average about 80,000 brick yearly to each man employed.

Brick-yards formerly worked, but idle for the last two or three years, are owned by Cochran & Russ, Suncook, and by James Thompson, Hooksett.

The brick-makers in Plaistow are as follows: Moses Goodchild, manufacturing about 1,000,000 brick yearly, employing 15 men; J. S. Lamprey, about 1,500,000, with 15 men; Isaac H. Pollard, 800,000, with 8 men; H. H. Cheney, 700,000, with 7 men; Isaac Hall, 500,000, with 5 men; George Denoncour, 1,000,000, with 10 men; D. Gauselain, 500,000, with 5 men; J. W. Porter, 500,000, with 5 men; Alack Janell, 1,000,000, with 10 men; Joseph Kimball, 500,000, with 5 men.

Bricks are made also at Dover Point, Rochester, Lebanon, Keene, Bedford, Boscawen, Bristol, Bartlett, Claremont, Haverhill, Concord, Durham, Epping, East Kingston, Francestown, Franklin, Greenville, Hampton, Hancock, Hillsborough, Jaffrey, Lancaster, Littleton, Merrimack, Moultonborough, Newport, Northumberland, Ossipee, Plymouth, Rindge, Rumney, Great Falls, Unity, Warren, Winchester, and Wolfeborough.

SOAPSTONE.

The Francestown Soapstone Company, with a capital of $300,000, has its mills for sawing at Nashua, and commenced operations, on a larger scale than had been employed hitherto, in May, 1866. The bed had been discovered originally by Mr. Daniel Fuller, in 1794, while engaged in ploughing. It was first wrought in 1802; and stone was transported to Boston for sale as early as 1812. Previous to 1866, about 2,000 tons of stone had been sold; 1,500 tons were sold in 1866, and 2,020 in 1867. The company made 3,700 stoves in 1867. I have no statistics of the extent of manufacture since this date; but the business is known to have been conducted upon a similar large scale ever since 1866. The refuse fragments and dust are also utilized, being ground and sold for packing.

I have visited this locality several times. The bed is regular, not nodular like the steatite and serpentine beds in Vermont. The opening is 80 feet long, 40 wide, and 80 deep, a little wider at the bottom than at the top. The bed has been followed for 400 feet in length. The peculiarity of the stone consists in the uniform distribution through it of spherical radiated aggregations of crystalline plates of talc. These make the stone uniformly strong in all directions, unlike most of the Vermont rock, which is apt to split along seams of original structure. The Francestown stone has largely superseded that from Vermont for the manufacture of stoves. I have already alluded to the dissemination of minute crystalline bits of pyrrhotite disseminated through the soapstone without seemingly injuring it.

The presence of radiated spherules marks this bed in its stratigraphical distribution. Other beds of it are found in Weare, Warner, Canterbury, and Richmond. The first named is near the top of Mt. Misery, and has been quite extensively opened by Hon. M. A. Hodgdon. I saw it first in 1869, and judged the bed to be 15 feet wide and quite hard. The stone had the same lithological features with that in Francestown, and occupies the same stratigraphical position. The excavation was about 10 feet deep. Two or three years later, the bed had been better defined by additional excavation. The hole in 1874 was seen to be 71 feet long and 60 feet wide, representing the width of the soapstone. Two or three large bunches of hard rock—horses—occur in it, one of them estimated to be 35 feet long. In going down there was seen, first, the common country rock, underlaid by a coarse-grained ledge with long hornblende crystals capping the soapstone. The latter rock is at the top inferior to that found lower down. Small bunches of granitic rock occurred occasionally; and the pyrrhotite showed itself in a vein three inches wide. The work was prosecuted far enough to determine the nature of the stone underneath the principal horse. The material was soft, but somewhat shelly. The great improvement in the appearance of the stone over what it was on the surface leads us to believe that good material will eventually be quarried here.

Mr. Hodgdon has also opened the ledge in the south-east corner of Warner, in the same bed, or its repetition by a fold. The bed is over 20 feet in width, and deserves to be opened more fully.

In Canterbury, this rock has been quarried near the Boston, Concord, & Montreal Railroad, a mile and a half south of the station. A hasty run over the ground showed the presence of two beds, each about 25 feet wide, separated by hornblendic rocks. One bed has been opened in two places. I have been unable to learn anything about the history of the work done here, and do not know why the quarry has been abandoned. It is very near a railroad, and conveniently situated for working. The stone is only partially like that from Francestown, occurring more like those in Vermont.

Circumstances have prevented such exploration of the country between Francestown and Canterbury as was anticipated. I have one impression of the relations of rocks to the soapstone that may be of value to others. The Canterbury bed lies just above a prominent belt of white feldspathic or granitic material. This may therefore be the guide to the occurrence of the soapstone. I have observed it in the west part of New Boston, and in Hopkinton. (See Vol. II, pp. 589, 159.)

Other localities of soapstone, of greater or less interest, are in Richmond, on land of Lorenzo Harris; boulders in Hampstead, Pelham, and Dracut, Mass.; and 1½ miles east of E. Hill's in Swanzey. This last named bed has not been mentioned heretofore, and is not located upon the map. I have no facts in regard to it to present.

Orford. Five beds of soapstone occur in this town, one in the Huronian, the others in the Coös mica schists. They are all of good quality. Some facts about them are found on pp. 382-4, in Volume II.

Haverhill. The soapstone quarry in Haverhill, now controlled by David Page, is situated about three miles north-east of North Haverhill station. It was first opened in 1855, and was worked up to the middle of the winter of 1857. About 150 tons were taken out and sent to market. The stone was pronounced to be of a fine quality for the first opening. The quarry then changed owners, and was not worked again until 1874, when some 50 or 60 tons of the stone were taken to market, and found to be of very good quality for all purposes for which soapstone is used. It is claimed that it can be brought to a finer edge than that from any other locality in the United States. It can be quarried in large quantities, and of almost any dimensions. The Boston, Concord & Montreal Railroad is 1½ miles distant.

Manufacture of Glass and Pottery.

Excellent materials for the manufacture of glass and pottery are abundant. The feldspar occurs in the coarse granite veins carrying merchantable mica. This range has been described in Volume II, page 514, extending from Easton to Surry, being of a fibrolite mica schist, and is admirably shown upon the map. At almost any part of this range these coarse granite veins are liable to occur. Masses of it a foot square are common wherever the veins have been opened. It is now thrown away because it cannot be utilized. Our feldspar has been successfully used in the manufacture of artificial teeth by several dentists. The time is coming when our immense supplies of feldspar will be utilized. We have no beds of kaolin or porcelain clay that are of value. Quartz, valuable for the manufacture of glass, is exceedingly common. The ranges of it which I have represented upon the map, and fully described in Volume II, are nearly all sufficiently pure for this purpose. These occur, first, through Hillsborough, Rockingham, and Strafford counties on the east, and from Cheshire to Grafton on the west side of the state. Very frequently there are large hills, hundreds of feet high and broad. In Lyndeborough there is an establishment fitted up for the manufacture of glass, based upon the presence of one of these beds of quartz. Although milky white, the quartz contains a small percentage of iron, and is therefore apt to impart a green color to the bottles manufactured. The iron is removed by first burning the stone in a kiln, so as to magnetize the hematite and limonite present; secondly, the brittle calcined rock is pulverized; thirdly and lastly, the powder is caused to fall over revolving cylinders bristling with magnets. These attract the iron, and thus purify the pulverized material, which is now ready to be put into crucibles. A very large business is done at Lyndeborough.

Mica.

Our state is celebrated for its mica. It occurs in enormous quantities, suitable for commercial use, in immense, coarse granite veins, where the three mineral constituents are found in large pieces. The mica I have seen in plates a yard long, but 10 or 12 inches is a more common size. On account of the great value of this mineral, we have taken special pains to learn where it is distributed, as it does not occur at hap-hazard any more than veins of the metals. Upon the map we have distinguished a mica schist with fibrolite, one of the supposed divisions of the Montalban group. It is usually about two miles wide, and reaches from Easton to Surry, with occasional interruptions. It is extraordinarily developed about Rumney and Hebron, spreading out to fill the space between the two great areas of porphyritic gneiss. Those who search for this mineral will find that the valuable deposits of mica are to be found chiefly within this fibrolite area as delineated upon the map, corresponding with that of the feldspar.

Quarries for mining mica have been opened in the following localities: In Grafton, the oldest and best known establishment is that of the Ruggles company, upon Isinglass hill. About 1840 they obtained some 600 or 700 pounds annually, valued at $1,500. In 1869 they marketed 75 boxes of 350 pounds each, worth from $2.15 to $2.50 per pound. This makes a total of 26,250 pounds, worth perhaps $60,000. In January, 1877, the Ruggles mine is said to have shipped 3,600 pounds of mica, selling for $2 per pound. They employed, in 1869, 12 men for seven months of the year. Within two or three years the price of mica has increased, and hence the business has been much stimulated. Grafton now has six openings, which are all worked. Mellen's quarry is about 700 feet above the valley, to the north of the Ruggles mine. There are six or eight places where excavations have been made. Martin & Page are at work energetically, near the top of Alger or Beryl hill. This is the locality where the largest known beryl was once on exhibition. These parties have worked here for two years. Another place is opened by Kilton & Sargent. On Hoyt hill in Orange is the Worcester mine. The vein shows for 400 or 500 feet near the hill-top, and its maximum width is 100 feet. Five men were employed here at the time of my visit. The largest plate of mica obtained here is 8 inches square. There are two other mines on the east side of the railroad in Grafton. There are others, in Alexandria, New Hampton, Wilmot, Marlborough, Acworth, Alstead, Groton, and Springfield. The Alstead quarry has been worked intermittently the past thirty years by Mr. James Bowers, who sold in 1840 one thousand dollars' worth to the Boston market. His quarry is on Beryl hill, a famous locality for the latter mineral. On Hall's farm in Groton are unusually large plates of mica, where no mining has been done. The Springfield locality has furnished beautiful and large tourmalines.

Those who drive about Springfield, Grafton, Orange, etc., cannot fail to see these veins on the hill-tops, whitening their crests and sides. The vein on Hoyt hill, Orange, is quite conspicuous on the right-hand side, as the cars near the summit from the south. Aaron's ledge in Springfield is a landmark 15 to 20 miles away. The range seems to terminate with the Colonel Sanborn hill in Springfield; but I have found limited patches of it, not shown upon the map, near George's mills. The mica of New Hampshire is extremely abundant, and there is no danger that the supply will be exhausted for many generations.

Plumbago.

This mineral is found in Goshen, Antrim, Bristol, Nelson, Hancock, Chester, Mt. Monadnock, Sutton, Barrington, Bedford, Troy, Walpole, Washington, Hillsborough, Keene, Wentworth, Orford, and elsewhere. It is not equal in quality to that obtained at Ticonderoga and other Laurentian districts, but sells readily for a second quality article, and is useful for the manufacture of crucibles. The most extensive mine is at Goshen, formerly owned by President Pierce. It is on the flank of Sunapee mountain, included in pyritiferous mica schist, and accompanied by radiated black tourmaline. The bed is small, and traversed by a better quality of the same mineral in cross veins. The amount raised and sold annually has varied greatly. In 1840 the yield was 20 tons. A few years later the product was greater; and the locality is capable of furnishing a larger supply, should it be called for.

The Antrim bed is irregular in thickness, varying from a few inches to two feet. The material is said to be soft and pure.

Few minerals are talked of more than plumbago by the farmers, as they often find it in an impure condition. A good article is free from grit, and can be readily cut with the knife without coming into contact with hard bunches. To those searching for it, I would recommend exploitation where the rocks are most crystalline. All our mica schists show the mineral, but it is apt to be impure.

Precious Stones.

These are not abundant; but very beautiful specimens of beryl, garnet, cinnamon stone, amethyst, rose quartz, iolite, and other minerals are often found, which are suitable for being cut as gems. I refer the reader to Part IV for a description of the minerals and localities.

Polishing Powder.

Chapter XIV, Volume I, is devoted to a description of the organisms, which by their decay give rise to the white, light earth sometimes called infusorial silica. It is liable to occur beneath any bog in the state. The few deposits we have are of excellent quality, and the quantity is sufficient for commercial use. The largest deposits are at Umbagog lake, Fitzwilliam, Stark, Tamworth, and on Stamp Act island, Wolfeborough. Others are known to exist at Bemis lake in Livermore, Littleton, Laconia, Bristol, Chalk pond in Newbury, Epsom, Bow, in a pond north-west from the Crawford house, White Mountains, Concord, Manchester, Durham, Grafton, and Exeter. The Fitzwilliam deposit is sold extensively for a polishing material. The principal use made of this article at the present day is in the manufacture of dynamite, and it commands a price of from $15 to $18 per ton. The most northern locality is in Cambridge, upon Umbagog lake, near W. M. Thurston's, where it occupies, in the lake, on the islands, and on projecting points of land, an area of fifty acres or more. It varies in depth from a few inches to two feet, although, as our observations were limited, the depth may be in places much greater. It is covered in the lake by a lacustrine deposit, and on the islands by an accumulation of soil.

In the town of Stark we find it in Pike's pond. It is here known to be three feet in depth, and it is probably much more. It seems to be distributed over the entire bottom of the pond.

Whetstones.

These are quarried in Piermont and Haverhill by Mr. Pike. I have not his figures for the number of stones produced; but the business is a large one, and the material is inexhaustible. Other towns along the Connecticut river contain the same rock.

Two localities of novaculite or oil-stone are capable of supplying plenty of oil-stones. One is upon Fitch hill in Littleton, near the Helderberg fossils; and the other is at the north base of the Ossipee mountains. The place may be known by the fact that certain dark streaks in the stone have been mistaken for the rocks accompanying coal. Parties interested in selling the "mine" procured bits of bituminous coal from a convenient blacksmiths' shop, and strewed them in the soil near this opening.

Ochres.

Bog-iron ores of the nature of ochre occur at Bow, Lancaster, Bedford, Amherst, Merrimack, Bath, Madison, Grafton, Lebanon, Barrington, Gilmanton, Mason, Lyndeborough, New Boston, Chesterfield, Nottingham, Orange, Pembroke, Salisbury, Jaffrey, Moultonborough, Orford, Surry, and Plainfield. One of the most extensive is upon the land of David Colby, in the west edge of Hooksett, where I saw a few hundred pounds of red and yellow paints that had been washed free from impurities and prepared for the market. The material seemed to be sufficiently abundant to be utilized. I have not seen the ochre manufactured into paint elsewhere in the state.

The other articles enumerated at the outset, viz., copperas, alum, titanium, and moulding-sand, can be obtained from various localities. The first could be manufactured at several localities in the Connecticut valley, though not so as to be able to compete successfully with the works upon Copperas hill.

CHAPTER III.

NATURAL FERTILIZERS.

THE rocks of New Hampshire are largely granitic or feldspathic. In decomposition an abundance of potash is liberated, together with variable quantities of soda and lime. But our soils invariably show a small percentage of phosphates universally distributed. As crystals of apatite are uncommon, the question has often arisen in my mind, Whence is this salt derived? We cannot believe that enough animals have left their skeletons during the later periods, when the present soil was in the process of formation, to explain the commonness of this essential ingredient. If not of animal, it must have been of mineral origin.

The statement has been made by prominent agriculturists, that our rocks generally contain phosphate of lime. One of the points aimed at in the microscopic study of our rocks has been a search for apatite, under the impression that the soil phosphate must exist in minute crystals, invisible to the naked eye. Our researches have shown the presence of this mineral in rocks from every part of the state. This fact gives us confidence in the ability of our underlying formations to furnish from age to age a plentiful supply of this salt, so essential to the growth of crops.

Part IV contains numerous incidental references to the localities of microscopic apatite. I will enumerate the instances there mentioned, presuming that they are much more abundant than are here indicated. It occurs in the porphyritic gneiss of Antrim, the ancient gneisses of

Westmoreland, Grafton, and Swanzey, various mica schists, the quartz schists of Portsmouth, the Huronian of Norwich and Hanover, the gabbro of the White Mountains, the diabases of Bemis brook and Rye, the augite sienite of Jackson, the sienites of Chatham and Red hill, the diorites of Campton, Stewartstown, and Dixville, and the granite of Rye, Concord, Colebrook, Lightning mountain, Jackson falls, and the coarse veins carrying the valuable masses of mica and feldspar. It is found, also, in the porphyry of Waterville and Albany, and in the town of Piermont.

The other natural fertilizers of importance are limestones and the various forms of peat. The first have been described already in the preceding chapter. It is astonishing that our farmers so entirely neglect the abundant supplies of limestone occurring in our midst, and either fail to procure this mineral, when required for their soil, or else purchase that which has been brought hundreds of miles.

Only two beds of calcareous marl are known in the state,—at Hollis and Columbia. Both are limited in amount, while the substance itself is of excellent quality.

Two and a half miles south-east of Colebrook village, in the north part of Columbia, is Lime pond. This pond is nearly a hundred rods long, and probably half as wide. Its bottom is covered with white calcareous marl, which has a depth in some places of 15 feet. On the east side of the pond there is also a buff-colored sedimentary deposit.

The marl is formed by the accumulation of myriads of shells of the Cyclas and Planorbis, an abundance of which was everywhere found where the marl was covered with water, for the pond has been partially drained. Dr. Jackson supposed the neighboring peat swamp to be the most active agent in supplying the shell-fish with calcareous salts, from which they secrete the carbonate of lime of their shells. "On testing the water, it was found to be charged with crenate, apocrenate, and humate of lime, and it contains, also, a notable proportion of ammonia. In evaporating a portion of the water, a buff-colored precipitate subsides, which contains the above-mentioned organic acids, combined with lime and an excess of carbonate of lime, which was originally held in solution by carbonic acid as a bicarbonate."

Peat is the vegetable soil of bogs and swamps, and consists of the dèbris of decomposed aquatic or marsh plants. That formed from moss is of the best quality, and it is very abundant in the granitic regions of the northern United States. Muck is peaty matter mixed with soil, and is consequently less valuable than the pure article. Peat ripens with age or advancement in decomposition, and is thus comparatively heavy and dense, and appears pitchy. Its value increases with age. This substance may make a good fuel; but especially it is susceptible, under proper treatment, of becoming a valuable fertilizer. It absorbs and retains water and ammonia, promotes the disintegration of the rocks, renders light soils more productive by its application, and acts as a direct fertilizer.

Those who have experimented with this material, and compared its properties with those of ordinary stable manures, find that it usually carries, in a given amount, one third more organic matter, an equal amount of lime and nitrogen, but is deficient in potash, magnesia, phosphoric and sulphuric acids. These deficiencies may be remedied by adding to 100 pounds of fresh peat one pound of commercial potash, or five pounds of unleached wood ashes, one pound of good superphosphate, or one pound each of bone-dust and plaster of Paris. In view of the small amount and the cheapness of the materials to be added to peat to make it equal to stable manure, it seems as if the farms of New Hampshire might be greatly enriched at a very small expense. The peat of various localities requires different degrees of amendment; and therefore only the general rule given above can be stated to show what ought to be done. Samples should be sent to a chemist for special analysis by those who wish to utilize the article.

Without speaking exhaustively, we have a few notes about peat in different localities, which may be of service in giving some idea of the great abundance of the deposit in every section of the state. The facts from the extreme north were furnished by Mr. Huntington, and others are copied from Mr. Upham's note-book.

Bogs and peat swamps are very numerous in northern New Hampshire. They are found in every town, and are often of great extent. Sometimes they present a broad area, without the vestige of a tree or shrub, except along their borders, and this area is covered with a luxuriant growth of grass (*Calamagrostis Canadensis*). One of the largest of this kind is a mile and a half west of Second lake, at the head of Bay brook, and it has an area of fifteen or twenty acres. West of Perry Stream, on the same line going west, there is another extensive bog; and also northward, near the head of the same stream, there are several. These are more or less occupied by shrubs and trees. The laurel, *Kalmia glauca*, labrador tea, and the *Ledum palustris*, are common, while here and there, from the sphagnous bed, rises a hackmatack or larch. Northward of Second lake, towards Mt. Carmel, there is a very extensive swamp, but there are no open bogs. Here, besides the laurel, the labrador tea, and the larch, we frequently find the cedar and the alder. Half a mile south of the south bay of Connecticut lake there are two small open bogs; and on these cranberries are abundant. These bogs, like those north, seem to have been formed almost entirely from a species of moss (sphagnum). The peat here is not more than six feet in depth, and for the most part it seems to be composed of partially decomposed fragments of the moss.

Organic acid produced by the vegetable matter, when long saturated in water, removes from the subsoil of the bogs the oxides of iron and manganese, as well as lime and other alkaline earths: hence the subsoil of bogs usually consists of bleached whitish sand and clay of a very unproductive character. There are few exceptions to this, in localities where the soil contains a very large proportion of lime. On the other hand, when the underlying rocks contain an iron sulphide, the sulphuric acid produced from this mineral gives a still greater degree of acidity to the bog, while the iron is sometimes in too great quantity to be entirely removed. "The iron and manganese, removed in the manner above mentioned, are deposited, usually, in rounded kernels at the outlet of such bogs, or in the soils through which the water soaks, and become partially exposed to the air. In this way small quantities of bog-iron ore and bog manganese ore are formed in the vicinity of many swamps. All these facts respecting bogs have their analogies on a large scale in our ancient rocks." "The bogs, when drained and their surfaces dressed with sand or sand and lime, to supply the siliceous and calcareous matter in which they are deficient, are excellent soils, second only to dyke marshes in their productiveness in hay and oats." There are many bogs in northern New Hampshire that might in this way be reclaimed, as it is not improbable that in time the peat from the swamps will be used as fuel and as a fertilizer. One of the most extensive swamps in the state is in the south-east part of the Dartmouth College grant. The distance across this bog on the state line is 290 rods, and the distance east and west, including the bogs on both sides of the Magalloway, is much greater. Along the Androscoggin there are several interesting peat deposits. One in Milan, just north of the mouth of the Chickwolnepy, has in it many trunks of fallen trees, principally tamarack (larch), nearly all of which are well preserved. In Shelburne, on the farm of Mr. Burbank, is a peat swamp that has been partially reclaimed.

The peat lands of Rochester, probably more than 150 acres in total amount, are well seen from the Portsmouth, Great Falls & Conway Railroad. The deepest soundings in these bogs, found by the railroad survey, were a little more than 20 feet. Between the village and the first crossing north is the most extensive single area. Here 50 to 60 acres, upon which the peat is 5 to 15 feet deep, situated on the east side of the railroad, are owned by the Strafford County Improved Peat Company. This company was incorporated during the civil war, when the price of coal was greatly advanced. After the war, coal was again cheap, so that it was thought impossible to prepare peat for the market at a profit, and no work was ever done by the company. Mr. E. J. Mathes has used this peat two or three years as fuel for his house. It is cut with a spade shaped like the Irish slane. The pieces are spread to dry, for which they need to be turned over after two or three days. In this way the water, to the extent of 75 per cent. of their original weight, is evaporated, and they shrink one third in size. Thus prepared, the peat is very spongy. A better process, also employed by Mr. Mathes, is to grind the peat and break up its vegetable fibers, in the manner that clay and sand are mixed for brick-making. Thus ground and moulded like bricks, pieces 4 by 6 by 8 inches in dimension shrink in drying to 2 by 4 by 6 inches, or to one fourth their original size. The peat thus prepared is compact and hard, requiring a hammer to break it. It yields a considerable amount of ashes, which are very light and dusty. They are found useful for polishing.

Several peat-bogs occur in Stratham. The largest is the Temple meadow in the south-east part of the town, covering 60 acres, the depth of peat averaging about 4 feet; its greatest depth is 6 feet. This peat has never been used. Another peat-swamp, occupying about 10 acres, lies one mile north of the village. This was used for fuel to some extent about fifty years ago. Its only use now is as a manure, for which about 100 cords are dug yearly. About half a mile east from the last is the Heath swamp, containing about 100 acres of peat. This was never used for fuel. About 50 cords are employed yearly for manure. The depth of peat in these swamps exceeds 20 feet.

Other localities, where peat is conspicuously abundant, are South Lancaster, Springfield, Grantham, Enfield, Lebanon, and many others in Rockingham, Strafford, Hillsborough, and Merrimack counties.

INDEX.

INDEX TO PART V.

ERRATA.

Part III.

On page 167, line 6 from the bottom, for "Plate IV," read *Plate VII.*

On page 184, line 5, for "Bronson hill," read *Bronson's kiln.*

On page 184, line 13, for "S. 28° E," read *S.* 28° *W.*

The same upon page 212, line 20.

On page 187, line 16, "Mrs. M. Gale's" should be placed under *Belmont.*

On page 187, line 35, "K. Hall's" should be placed under *Gilford.*

On page 187, lines 4 and 5 from the bottom, for "south corner," read *Strafford Corner.*

On page 188, last line, for "Newbury," read *Sutton.*

On page 189, line 15 from the bottom, "E. C. Sanborn's" should be placed under *Hampton Falls.*

On page 194, lines 6 and 7 from the bottom, "Lufkin's and Howe's" should be placed under *Rumford.*

On page 202, last line, insert "not" before distinguishable.

On page 203, line 11, for "south-east," read *south-west.*

On page 302, first line, for "rounds," read *mounds.*

Part IV.

On page 8, line 8 from the bottom, for "clacite," read *calcite.*

On page 80, line 7 from the bottom, for "Fig. 2 on Pl. 9," read *Fig.* 9 *on Pl.* 2.

On page 102, in the formula, for "Al," read Al^2.

On page 15, and elsewhere in the first chapter, for "pinnacoid," read *pinacoid.*

Part V.

On page 44, line 7 from the bottom, and page 45, line 26, for "slums," read *slimes.*

www.ingramcontent.com/pod-product-compliance
Lightning Source LLC
LaVergne TN
LVHW011119110826
845150LV00008B/2190
* 9 7 8 1 4 2 5 5 7 2 0 6 8 *